# Shouted

# Whispers

## By Susan Romayne Andrus Clark

# Table of Contents

# Shouted Whispers

Looking up at the sound of a car pulling in the driveway drew my attention away from the news on the idiot box. I jammed the remote off and flung the remote on the couch. *"Thank God, Jack[1] was not active in the 50s,"* I thought.

"We have company," I called to Mom as I stood up and walked to the back of the house to open the kitchen door. "It's Kath and Mike." Noticing that they had two cars and Mike backed his car in, I reached up and opened the garage door. As I did this, Mom came into the kitchen and started making coffee.

I opened the back door. "Hi," I called as I stepped out on the cement platform between the house and the garage.

The second car had pulled up the driveway and parked in the turnaround. Mike was already out of the red Buick LaSabre, and he was helping my sister, Kathleen, get out. He had backed the car in so they could hook their trailer hitch to the hitch of their car.

"Hi," he called.

Kath stood up, but she was unable to lift her head for the first few steps she took; then, with a shrug-like jerk, she lifted her head. She waited for Mike to get her respirator out of the car and finished walking towards the garage.

"Hi Suz," she said in a voice barely audible because of being on a respirator and from post-polio syndrome. Their three boys, Eric, Michael, and Geof, were getting out of Elic's old blue Oldsmobile. "We came to get the trailer so the

---

[1] Jack Kevorkian, a well-known physician and advocate of euthanasia.

1

boys could pack it to go back to school." The three boys lifted the trailer tongue, pulled the open box trailer toward the car, and slid the tongue onto the hitch on the back of the car. In just minutes, they had the trailer hooked up and were ready to leave.

Eric, the oldest and biggest, called to me, "Thanks, Aunt Sue."

"You're welcome," I called back. The other boys hooked up the lights, while Mike pulled Kath's gray athletic bag out of the car trunk, shut it, and motioned for the boys to leave.

Then, Kath, Mike, and I walked toward the house.

"Come on in," I held the kitchen door open for Kath, and Mike held the door and motioned for me to go in.

"Do you have time to do Kath's hair?" he asked.

"Sure," I replied as we walked into the kitchen.

"What are you kids up to?" Susan and Kathleen's mother, Marion asked.

"Oh, the boys are getting ready to go back to Ferris, and they want to use the trailer to haul things in," Mike said as he tossed the newspaper on the table. Everyone knew Mom liked reading the paper, but she refused to keep a subscription to it. Since the boys always had a paper route, they would bring the daily paper for Grandma to read when they came. Even the neighbor brought one over when she was done reading it.

"Well, come on in and sit down for a while," Mom said as she put cups of coffee on the table.

Mike gave Kath's bag to me, put his pipe on the table, and then sat down in the master chair at the end of the table by the back door.

I opened the bag and began getting the items needed to do Kath's hair.

"We're going to Ferris on Sunday, and I wanted my hair done for it," Kathleen said.

"What did you say?" Mom asked.

Mike repeated for Kathleen, "We're going to Ferris on Sunday, and Kath wanted her hair done so she can fool the kids there."

As Mike continued to tease Mom, I prepared the solution to color Kath's hair. With her foot, Kath pulled the chair from the wall and sat down. She was having a harder time lifting her head than the last time I did her hair. It was too bad that the doctors couldn't discover a way for her to hold her head up that didn't make it harder for her to breathe. When she first had polio, she had a brace that worked; why not now? Even though the brace that they had tried to use recently made it harder for her to breathe, I was glad to know that she was going to the doctors and trying to get help. While working on Kath's hair, I reminisced about when we all had polio.

***

It was before Thanksgiving when they came and took Kath to the hospital. I was just six years old, but I remember fearing going to school that day. It seemed like I would never see her again. On the way to school, I remember seeing the ambulance coming to the house from the back seat of the school bus. When I got home from school that day, I ran to the bedroom only to see she wasn't there. All of us knew she was very sick. All seven of us children had polio in some form.

For me, polio felt like cold weights inside me. Because every muscle was heavy and did not want to move, I felt weak and wanted to crumple like a rag doll. I ached all over, and every time I climbed out of the covers, I was so cold that I shivered. The blue fuzzy blanket on my bed would be pulled into whatever room I wanted to go into, and I would go from bed to register as soon as I heard the furnace come on. When the furnace turned off, I would run back to the bed because it was too cold to stay out of bed. Sometimes, even when I was in bed, it was too cold.

One morning, I felt too weak to get up very often, and I remember standing in the hall between the kitchen and bedroom. I was afraid because I thought I would be like Kath and not be able to get up again. My oldest brother was standing there, also, and keeping my voice low so Mom wouldn't hear me, I said, "Skip, I'm afraid. It's hard to get up anymore, but I don't want to be like Kath. What can I do?"

"Make yourself get up no matter what. That's what I did, and I finally got over it."

"But sometimes it's so cold and so hard to move."

"Make yourself move no matter what!" he whisper-shouted at me so Mom wouldn't hear. He pointed a finger at me, "Use your brain and make yourself move no matter what!" He scared me.

So, I made myself move somehow. Even when it was cold. And it worked. Within days, I was stronger and not feeling the cold. The more I moved, the stronger I felt. Soon all of us were back at school except for Kath. She was still in the hospital weeks later.

4

One night, Mom and Dad were at the hospital visiting Kath, and the rest of us were home trying to catch up on our homework. All of us were sitting around the kitchen table with papers in front of us. Skip, the oldest, was at the A & P store working as a bagger and stock person.

Karen, the oldest of us five, was walking from one to the next and helping us with our homework. She had Betty Jane's vocabulary list in her hand.

"How do you spell shopping?" she asked as she looked at Jerome's math. "This one is right, but this one is wrong," she pointed out on his paper.

"What'd I do wrong?" he asked. He was sitting at the head of the table where Dad usually sat and was across from Betty Jane.

Sitting in Mom's chair, Betty Jane's head bobbed down as she wrote the word on the paper. Ray sat behind the table and against the wall and was quietly working on a report for one of his classes.

"Can we have some popcorn?" I asked. My chair was turned on an angle at the side of the table so I could kneel at times as I wrote out my vocabulary words, but I would also not be in Karen's way as she walked around the table.

"Do you have your homework done?" Karen looked at the paper in front of me. I liked making my letters carefully, so my paper looked neat, and I held it up for her to look at.

"Show off," Jerome said.

The others laughed, and I said, "What'd he say?"

"Never mind," Karen said. "When Jerome gets his homework done, the popcorn will be ready." She went downstairs where the popper was kept, brought it up, plugged it into the outlet on the stove behind me, and put the grease in the popper pan to melt. It was one of those poppers that had two parts to it. The bottom pan was a metal case that had the element in it, and the top was a metal bowl with a lid that fit snugly on top. She put the pan part on top of the element and started going for the popcorn in the refrigerator.

"Karen, does this sound right?" Ray asked. "By placing the wires..." he read from his paper.

My knees were getting sore, so I stretched my legs out in front of me. I didn't feel like listening to his report, and it sounded boring. Karen was standing next to Ray behind the table and looking at his paper as he read it to her.

"It sounds pretty good to me, but I think you need to look at some of the commas and check to see if they are being used right," Karen said when he finished reading it.

"Come'ere, Karen, is this right?" Betty Jane asked.

Karen went over to him, and I looked up as she passed by me to stand between us.

Something smelled funny. "Karen! The popcorn!" I yelled.

She grabbed the pan, lifted it out of the base, and pulled the lid off in one quick motion. Immediately it burst into flames and caught her hair on fire, so she dropped the pan; and with her hands, she beat at her hair to stop the flames.

"Ray! Get the neighbor!" she hollered.

The pan landed on the floor between the stove and my chair, and as it hit the floor, some of the grease and flames hit my tights and started melting them. I pulled my legs up tight, but the flames were too high and started burning my arms.

I thought, if I go to the right, the pan is right there and I'll be burnt worse; but I can't go to the left because the chair is wedged against the table; if I go under the table, my face will get burnt, and I don't want that!

Not knowing what to do, I turned around and climbed on the chair, but it hit my legs more; so I hollered, "Karen! Help!"

She had been standing by Betty Jane behind me and was putting the fire out of her hair. All of a sudden, I felt like I was flying through the air, and I was up in her arms away from the fire. The back door opened behind me, and I could feel the cool breeze against my hot skin. Behind me, I could hear a loud hiss, but I couldn't see what was going on. Karen kept saying, "I'm sorry, Susan, I'm sorry."

The next-door neighbor, Mrs. Kelly, said, "Let's take a look and see." She stepped around the pan still on the floor and started taking my clothes off.

"Not in here," I said; "The boys are in here."

They took me to the bedroom and started pulling what was left of my tights off. "Ow! Stop, that hurts!" I pulled at Karen to get away from Mrs. Kelly.

Karen held me close and said, "Just be brave, Suz, just be brave."

"Oh my God!" Mrs. Kelly said.

"Com'on Suz; we have to get them off."

We'll do it quickly; then it won't hurt so long," Mrs Kelly said.

"Owwwww!" I cried.

Karen held me until it was done and kept saying, "I'm sorry, Suz!"

I looked up at Karen, and she had as many tears on her face as I had on mine. I had never seen Karen cry before, so I asked, "Are you hurt, Karen?"

"No," she replied, "I just don't like to see you hurt."

Then they wrapped me in Mom's pink chenille robe. Mrs. Kelly buttoned the robe up, looked at Karen and said, "She has to go to the hospital. Where are your parents?"

"Up visiting Kathleen," Karen replied.

"Which one?" Mrs. Kelly asked.

"She is at St. Luke's. We should go there," Karen replied.

"I want to go where Mom and Dad are," I said.

As Mrs. Kelly and Karen looked at each other, Mr Kelly called them to go into the kitchen. It seemed scary in the bedroom by myself, so I was glad when they came back in.

"OK," said Mrs. Kelly as Mr. Kelly walked in behind her. "Is there anything you need?"

The pain had stopped, but I was still shivering, but as long as I was going to be by Mom and Dad, I felt better.

I asked, "Can we go in the T-Bird? All the other kids have had a turn riding in it but me."

"You can go in any car you want," Mr. Kelly said.

Karen picked me up in her arms, and we went through the kitchen. It still smelled like burnt hair and smoke, but the fire was out, and the pan was in the sink. The element was still on the stove, but it was no longer plugged in. Everyone wanted to be the one to go to the hospital, and Mrs. Kelly said, "We should have an adult go to the hospital and one stay here with the rest of the kids." Since his white T-Bird did not have a back seat and the front seat was only two bucket seats, we were limited.

"I'm driving the car, so you need to figure out who will go along," Mr Kelly said.

"Karen, I'd like you to go with me," I said.

"I will stay with the rest of the kids then," Mrs. Kelly said as we walked out the door.

It was only thirty feet from our back door to their carport. Even though I had Mom's warm robe on, the cool night air doused the fire on my arms and legs until the burning was almost gone.

When we got to the car, Mrs. Kelly said, "Let me hold you until your sister gets in the car." Karen squeezed in on the soft white leather seat that went woosh as she sat on it, and I was put on her lap.

"What's the hospital like, Karen?" I asked.

"It's a place where they help people get better. Just be brave and everything will be okay," she replied.

I thought about Skip's idea of using my brain. It helped me then, so I thought about feeling better.

The night was cool, and I was still a little afraid, but I was also excited about riding in the car. I kept looking around. The dash was polished plastic that looked like wood. I recognized the stick shift that Dad would sometimes let us shift when we were on dirt roads. It was on the floor between the seats, so Karen kept pulling me away from the middle of the car.

"Does it hurt a lot?" Karen asked.

"No."

"Why are you shaking then?"

I had not realized I was even shaking.

"I don't know. I guess I'm just scared but also excited about riding in this car." Before we even realized it, we were at the hospital. Karen stayed by me all the time, and I was glad she was there with me. As soon as we got there, Mr. Kelly went up to tell Mom and Dad what happened, and Karen and I were settled into the emergency room stall. The nurse gave me some patient gowns to put on. I had to put one with the open side in the back and the other like a robe, so my back was covered. Then the nurse gave me a white blanket to cover up with. I was not cold, but I still had not stopped shaking. There were many people in white running around. Even though the room smelled like chemicals, I could still smell the smoke from the fire. Everything looked like it was white except for the metal in the room. A beige curtain separated our stall from the next one, and I could hear a boy crying and screaming somewhere beyond that curtain.

"He must be very hurt," I said to Karen.

She let go of my hand and peeked around the curtain. Then she came back over to the cart I was lying on and said, "It's a boy older than you, and he has a cut lip. The doctor is trying to sew it up."

"That must hurt a lot. Have you ever had stitches?"

"No, but I know it doesn't hurt as much as this must. You are being very brave." Thinking of Skip and using my brain, I said, "This doesn't really hurt that much. It's just scary being here. There's Mom!"

She came in with Dad right behind her. Almost at the same time, the doctor came in from the stall next to ours. He looked at Mom and Dad and asked, "Is it okay for us to treat her?"

He brushed some hair from the front of his face. Mom and Dad nodded, and he came over by my cart. "I'm not going to do anything right now, but let me take a look at what you have here." Gently, he lifted the covers off, and Karen helped him move the hospital gown so he could see.

"What's wrong with the boy?" I asked.

"What you have here is much more serious than what's in the other room."

"Go ahead and take care of him and help him stop crying. I'll be okay. Mom and Dad are here, and I'll be okay."

He stopped and looked at me, "This doesn't hurt that much?"

I shook my head.

He looked at Mom and Dad, "It must be that the air temperature is just right. I'll be back in a few minutes."

The next few minutes were hectic. While Karen explained what happened, the nurse brought in a tray with some things that the doctor wanted. Then Mr. Kelly came in, and Mom told Karen to go home with him. Before I knew anything else, the doctor was in and was cleaning the burns. Before this, I had not wanted to look at them; but while he worked, I could see how much was burnt. Both of my legs had parts of tights stuck to them, and he worked at cutting them away from the blisters. There were burns on both of my arms where I had put them around my legs to shield them from the flames. When the doctor finished putting the medicine on and wrapping me up, both my arms and both my legs were wrapped up. My left side was not as wrapped as my right, and it was hard to bend my arms or legs. While he was working on me, he kept asking questions to Mom and Dad, but I couldn't keep up with the conversation.

Finally, he said, "That'll do it, I think. We have to keep you here for a little while, Susan. You'll be in with other children."

"Will I be in with my sister?"

He looked over at my parents, who shook their heads. Dad said, "She is in an iron lung."

"No," the doctor replied, "That's a different part of the hospital, but you will be in with many other children, so you will be able to make some new friends."

"I would rather be with my sister."

"I'm afraid we can't do that. Your sister has a big machine that she needs, and there's not much room for other things in there."

"That's okay, doctor. She'll be fine just where you want her," Mom said.

"Well, I'd like to talk to you outside for a few minutes if I may." He turned to me and said, "They'll be right back, and the nurse will be here with you until they do."

After that, things happened pretty fast. The nurse gathered my robe and shoes and put them at the foot of the cart. By the time Mom and Dad were back, she was ready to take me up to my room.

That night, I had a hard time going to sleep. I kept hearing the baby on the floor below us cry. She must have been a very tiny baby because her voice sounded like that, and I wondered why someone didn't pick that little baby up and help her. Mom would never let a baby cry like that. She cried and cried. I never knew why. The nurse came in with a flashlight and shined it on all of us. It hit my face, and I had to shut my eyes; it was so bright.

"You're still awake?" She looked at her watch. "It's 3 AM. What's the matter?"

"Why don't they take care of that tiny crying baby? I can hear her through the floor."

"What do you mean?" Her voice revealed concern.

"Listen, I can hear her crying through the floor. She has been doing that for a long time[2]."

"You just go back to sleep. I'll take care of the crying for you." She did, too. It wasn't very long after that, the baby stopped crying, I felt better and was soon asleep.

The next day, the nurses came in right after breakfast and told me that they had to move me to another room. I wondered for a long time if it was because of the fuss I made that night.

I always liked the next room. It was right over the front door to the hospital, and I could see all the people coming and going. Most of the time, I was in the room by myself because I was in isolation, and Mom would take turns seeing me and Kath. Because Mom had to put on a hospital gown, gloves, and a mask, she didn't come to see me as much as I wanted her to. She said it made it hard to breathe in the mask.

---

[2] In the 1950's there was a general practice of abortion doctors to leave the babies who survived the abortion process in the bedpan in a closet until they died from exposure.

13

I could not go down to the playroom because they feared the chance of infection, so most of the time I played with the books Mother would bring to me.

Other people didn't like coming into the room because they had to put the gowns on, too. Even the nurses didn't like it. One time, there was a nurse who put me on a bedpan and left because I was taking so long to go. Then when I was finished, I pushed the call button, but she didn't come in. I pushed the button a second time, and someone else answered, "Can I help you?"

"I need to get off the bedpan."

"Okay, I'll send someone down to you," but this person never showed up.

I was glad to be able to look out the window and watch all the people coming into the hospital, and this kept me busy for a while. Some would come in very slow and even hesitate before they came in the door. One nurse did not, though. She looked very nice. She had a smile, long curly brown hair, and a neat white uniform on, and each time she stepped up a step, she seemed to bounce. I hoped she would work on our floor for the rest of the day. Then there weren't so many coming in, and my tailbone started hurting. It hurt to sit on that thing for too long. I waited until I thought enough time had passed for the nurse I had seen coming in through the window would make it up to our floor, and I pushed the call button again.

"Can I help you?" the metal box on the wall squeaked. "Will someone please come and get me off this bedpan?"

"Are you still on that thing?" the box relayed.

"Yes, please hurry, it hurts."

When the nurse I saw from the window came in, I said, "I'm so glad it's you working from now on today. I saw you come in, and I waited until I thought you would get up to this floor, and I knew you would help me."

"Well, turn over, and I'll get it out." She helped me turn, and the pan stuck to my skin, so she had to pull on it to get it off, and it spilled.

"You have a bright red ring here from this! How long have you been on this anyway?"

"I don't know. I was on it when I saw you come in the hospital door down there."

"You've been on this that long?" she asked while she changed the wet sheet.

"Yes." I was glad that it didn't spill on any of the dressings on my legs, and she didn't have to change them. Whenever they took the bandages off, the burns would sting and hurt until long after they put the new bandages on again.

"Okay. Are you settled in now?" she asked when she was finished.

"Just great! Thanks!"

Shortly after that, the nurse who put me on the pan came in.

"What did you have to tell them for?" she said as she grabbed a book from my hand. "They told me to come in here and apologize to you, but you're…"

The door opened and interrupted her. The nice nurse poked her head in and said,

"Enough! Get out here!" I never saw the nurse who put me on the pan again.

In the next few days, many things happened that I didn't understand. In that time, they did many tests on me. They poked me with needles to get blood, to put IVs in, but the worst to get through was one day on the day shift.

The doctor came in and started to explain what they were going to do to me. The only thing I understood was that they were going to put a big needle in my back, and I had to lie very still. Suddenly, there were about four or five doctors and three or four nurses coming into the room. They were not only dressed in green isolation gowns, but all of them also had paper caps, gloves, and masks, so all I could see were their eyes. So many people dressed this way scared me more than the idea of another needle.

Thinking about what Skip had said to me, I said, "I will be very good and lie still. You don't need so many people to hold me down."

"I know you'll be very good because you usually are; but they are here to learn, not to hold you down."

One of the nurses showed me how she wanted me to lie on my left side with my knees curled and tucked under my chin as far as I could get them to go because of the bandages. Then they opened the gown in the back and put something cold on my spine that made me shiver.

"Try to hold still," he said.

"I am." My voice sounded muffled even to me because my knees were in my cheeks.

"It's cold."

"Susan, just hold real still, now. I'm going to put the needle in."

In a more distant voice, I could hear, "Notice how I put the needle between the bony prominences."

The needle felt like a log in my back when it first went in, then I didn't feel anything from it, and I thought it wouldn't be too bad; but then he started moving it around, and that hurt; but I ground my teeth together and kept still. His voice kept droning on about what he was doing, and I hurt each time he moved it. I wanted him to get done, but it seemed to take so long. Every now and then, he stopped, and it didn't feel so bad when he talked, but then it moved, and it hurt again. I could feel the tears rolling down my face and the palms of my hands were all sweaty because I was holding them together so tight. Even the bandages began having a sweaty, musty smell. I couldn't help it, but I started to shake after a while. The nurse who was helping me hold the position finally said something to him.

Then the doctor put his gloved hand on the back of my shoulder and said, "Hold on, one more minute."

There was a sharp pain as the needle moved, and then the log slid out. The nurse let me go and sat back on her chair. I scooted up to the corner of my bed and pulled the sheet way up around me. The doctors started saying something to me, and all I could say was, "Go away." The doctors and nurses all marched out together except for the nurse who had held me down.

She sat in the chair by the bed for a minute, trying to calm me down. "That was a hard one to get through." Her hands were shaking almost as much as mine were. "It's all done now, they are gone from the room, and you can relax." She coaxed me from the corner and said, "It is important that you try to lie flat here. You will not get a headache if you keep your head down here." She pulled the pillow closer to me and patted the top of it. "Is there anything I can get for you?"

"My bandages stink; can you change them?"

"Of course." As she started getting the bandages ready, she started asking me about school, and I started feeling better.

After a few days in that room and in isolation, two nurses came in and asked if I wanted to see my sister.

"Of course!" I exclaimed as I shoved the books off my lap.

The first nurse said, "Now, you may expect her to be like the sister you had at home, but she has changed. So, we want to make sure this is what you want to do."

"I'm sure! Let's go."

The second nurse said, "We have to make sure you are not going to get an infection, so we have to wrap you up, and you have to stay in the wheelchair while we are out of the room."

"Okay."

I climbed into the wheelchair, and the bandages were double-checked to make sure they were wrapped over all the burns. They made sure the blue and white hospital gown was put on backwards as a robe. Then they put a blanket over my lap and legs.

"Try to keep your hands and arms under the blanket so they won't get infected," one of the nurses said behind me as we wheeled out of my room.

This was the first time I was allowed out of my room, so I gawked all the way to the elevator. There were machines and carts in the hall, but I looked in the rooms to see other children. Some were in their rooms, but not many. Most of them were in the playroom across from the nurses' station. Some were playing with clay, some with books, and others with building blocks. I couldn't wait until I was permitted to go in there. We got on the elevator, and I hated the feeling in my stomach as it started moving up. I was glad when it stopped, and we went down another hall to Kath's room.

It was a large room that had two big shiny metal machines in it, with a beige curtain between the two machines. Each machine was like a very large tin can turned on its side, and was plugged into the wall, and made breathing hissing sounds. There were no labels on the cans. Instead, there were long rectangular windows on each side that allowed the nurses to see into the cans. Inside each of the windows were two white circles of cloth-like material. There was a space under the can and then a shelf where a motor sat. Each can had four legs, and at the bottom of the legs were large wheels. At the front end of the can, Kath's head was sticking out of one of the cans and lying on a platform with a pillow under her head. Her hair was all wavy under her, and I have always envied her for her beautiful wavy hair. Her face looked so pretty there. There was a mirror angled over her face so that she could look at the things going on around her.

I could barely hear Kath whisper, "Bring her closer so I can see her legs."

"Remember what we said about her getting an infection; we can't let her get too close," the nurse behind my chair said.

'I want to see her legs," Kath whispered.

19

"Hi Kath," I said. "I'm okay. I'm just on the floor downstairs. Mom comes and sees me too."

"I know. Stand up," she whispered.

I started to stand up, but the nurse stopped me.

"No," she said. "We can't risk an infection."

Not knowing what an infection was, I wasn't afraid of it, but I didn't understand why she wanted me to stand up. "What do you need, Kath?"

"Just stand up. Can you stand?" she whispered.

"Yes, I can. Let me show her, please!" I looked at the nurses standing there. One nodded, so I pulled the blanket off and stood at the feet of the wheelchair.

"See, I can stand just fine. Don't worry, Kath, I'll be as good as new in a couple of days."

I could see that she was crying hard but not making a sound. Her nose was running, and I wanted to get a tissue for her, but the nurse was on my shoulder.

Finally, she got her next words out, "Pull the plug, Suz."

"What?"

"Take her out of here," Kath's nurse said.

"Pull the plug, Suz," Kath whispered.

I looked at Kath, but the nurses were getting me back in the chair and out the door before I could understand what she wanted.

"What did she want?" I asked my nurse.

"We'll take care of anything she needs, so don't worry. She'll be fine." The nurses had me off the elevator before I even realized we were on it. I had been excited to see Kath on the way, but now I was more scared than anything. It would be a long night before I could talk to Mom about it in the morning.

Even after talking to Mom, I didn't understand what Kath wanted. I didn't understand until I heard my brothers talking about it at home. Even then, I didn't understand because I didn't understand what death was. I was out of the hospital in just a few weeks, but Kath stayed in the hospital until Easter.

***

Reminiscing as I stand on a step stool behind Kath, I see her hair is as beautiful now as it was then, but now it gets colored like many of us our age do. All three of her boys have beautiful hair. I understand Kath's tears and frustration. Yes, I color her hair and do many things for her that others do for themselves, but I see three healthy boys who were born after Kath got out of the hospital, after she learned how to walk again, after she went back to school, and after she married Mike. I know she still wants me to pull the plug on her respirator. I, too, know of suffering. But I know of no suffering that would be worth losing those three boys, or allowing them to lose their mother, her knowledge, or her love.

# Post Polio Syndrome

```
                post        polio       syndrome
        m
        i                   iron
        r                   lung
         r                                          p
faces   o                                           u
         r   the    human    tin    can            l
             w                f             e        l
             e                r             x
             a                a             i        p
             k                i             s        l
             n                l             t         u
             e                t             e          g
             s                y             n
             s                           c          please !
                                          c
```

# Tiny Crying Baby

Do you hurt like I do?

Itchy bandages hold

Stopping any movement

Pulling every time, eating, or getting on bedpans

Monsters in ash green suits walk in without faces.

Their needles and fingers

Probing, pulling burnt skin

Raw meat burns as air hits

Pain stops hours later

Nights are long with noises

Your cry comes through the floorboards

Forcing the hurt deeper, tiny crying baby,

Nurse's light probes darkness

Startled by open eyes

"It's three am, you're awake?"

Why do they not hear you, tiny crying baby?

# Scientific Kanükaze

A relief living without it

Jack can fix it

It won't hurt

WAIT A MINUTE

Just push this button

Jack makes things simple

It will stop the nightmare

ONE MORE MINUTE

Preventing the worst

Jack gives a way

Ceasing the smell of rotting flesh

WAIT MOMMY

pathologist

scientist

god

DON'T GO MOMMY!!!

# Don't Mess Up In The First Place

Putting the tablecloth into the box in the trunk, Meredith noticed a box of matches and grabbed them along with the lighter fluid to light the fire in the pit later that night. She had always loved camping and learned as much as she could about the various campgrounds. She had even done some searching on the web for more information about others, but this was her favorite place to camp. The river made a big bend that almost circled the campground; tubers would get on the river just a few minutes walk upriver from the camping area and then ride the river until they were beyond the campgrounds.

Then, they would get out of the river to do it all over again.

Meredith wanted to get things unpacked so that she could sit down by the river and watch the tubers as they rode past the swimming area or stopped to tease the little kids playing in the shallow water. She put the matches and the can of lighter fluid next to the fire pit for later and took a sip of coffee from the Styrofoam cup on the table.

It was more of a small sound inside her head that Meredith heard. She looked up to see who was around, but the guys next door were in deep discussion about farming, and she could hear Paige, the neighbor's wife, in her camper doing supper dishes.

A little bit louder this time, the voice carried a sense of fear and urgency even though the words could not be made out. Meredith looked in various directions, but she was getting mixed signals. Her reasoning told her the problem was down by the river at the swimming hole, but the urgency seemed to be coming from the campground further upstream from the swim area. She started walking toward the end of the campground and upriver and could make out the words more clearly.

A woman's voice could just barely be heard, "Where's my baby?"

More of a screech than a question, the voice's urgency sharpened Meredith's attention, and she turned her head to hear more acutely what direction it came from. Increasing her pace, Meredith began moving off the curved drive through the park and onto the grass toward the river upstream from the swimming hole.

"My baby! Where's my baby!"

The voice came more clearly to Meredith, and in the distance, she could see several people wandering around the copse of poplars by the river's edge. There were several who seemed to be looking in the water, and some more looking in the brush around the trees. Meredith was running as fast as her chubby legs could move her body by this time. As soon as she could get a breath, she called to one of the men near her.

"A child is lost?"

"Yes," a man in a blue checked, short-sleeved shirt replied. "A boy about four or five, they say."

"How long ago?" she asked.

"About fifteen or twenty minutes ago. Have you seen one wandering up by the park entrance?"

"No, but where did he disappear?" Her mind was mentally calculating how far the child could have floated downstream in twenty or twenty-five minutes. Time seemed to move so quickly just before the children disappeared, but so slowly before they were found again.

"Just up by the sand bar where the camping area begins upriver."

"There are many looking up by there?"

"Yes, we've been looking all over there, and we've told the mother that we know he's not over there."

"Okay, keep looking there, but I think he will be more over this way. I'll check closer to the swimming area."

Meredith was running before the last words were out of her mouth. Not used to this kind of exertion, she could feel a stinging sensation in her chest as the air rapidly flowed through her, but she ignored it. If the child had been in the water and had a cramp, he would have doubled up, and the current would have pulled him at least this far in the river.

She ran past the campers and people sitting around them. Not sure if she was right in her figuring, she did not want to have all the people riled up over here. The riverbank sloped swiftly, and she almost fell going down the incline, but she regained her balance and stumbled into the water with her shoes on. There was nothing in the river in front of her, but she could just barely make out a brown lump in the water that might be a figure just past the swimming area on the opposite bank. By this time, others had caught up to her and were asking her what was going on.

"The lost boy!"

She pointed to the figure in the river, and said, "Tell them he's here!"

Running across the rocky riverbed, she lifted her feet high so that there would be less drag. When the water got too deep, she tried to spring over as much as she could for distance and to catch up with the body she saw floating ahead of her. He was headed for the deeper, more rapid water, so she began swimming.

Keeping her head and face toward the boy so she could keep her eyes on him, she lunged toward him and grabbed onto his arm that was dragging behind his body in the current. Then she pulled with all her might. Even though he was just a small boy, she was getting tired, and she was way out of shape for this kind of thing.

*"Where are all of the guys who could do this without even flinching?"* she wondered.

She pulled him to the middle of the river and was able to regain a foothold. Recalling her training in first aid, she tried to give the boy a few deep breaths, but she didn't have enough air in her own lungs to pass any on. To give herself some time to catch her breath, she decided to make sure he would not aspirate any of his stomach contents when she did CPR, so she pressed on his stomach just below the rib cage. Immediately, he emptied his stomach in the river, and she wiped his face off. She looked up at the other side of the bank to the swimming hole and saw about fifteen people standing there looking at her.

"Help me!" she barely breathed out.

When no one moved, she stopped moving and called out louder, "Help me!"

The man in the blue checked shirt ran into the water toward her and grabbed the boy from her.

"Take him up and lay him on the ground," she said as she gasped for breath. Her muscles were shaking and weak, and it was hard to put one foot in front of the other.

28

The man easily lunged through the water and had the boy on the bank before she took two steps in the water. "Start CPR on him," she called. They had him up on the hill, so she could not see what they were doing to him as she climbed up the bank. There were so many people around him that she could not see anything.

Meredith could hear the mother crying and calling, "My baby! My baby!" as she started poking her way between the people. In the middle of the circle of people, the mother was on her knees and cradling the boy in her arms.

"Doesn't anyone know CPR?" Meredith asked.

All of the people standing there just stared at her like she was speaking a foreign language. "No one knows CPR?" she repeated. "Help me then." She pointed at the man in the blue checked shirt. "You get to the manager and get an ambulance here. She pointed to another and said, "You get the people back from the middle here. Mom, give me your boy so I can help him."

Tears streaming down her face, the mother shook her head and moaned, "No. No."

"You have to give him to me so I can help. Here, let's lay him on the ground here and you can help me by getting him a blanket to warm him up with, and a pillow for his head. Quickly, go!"

Glad to have something to do that would help her little boy, the mother jumped up and ran to her friend and said, "Help me get these."

With the mother gone, Meredith was able to get started on the boy, and gave him some quick breaths, then she started pressing on his chest like she was trained to do. Count compressions first and then a breath. Repeating this cycle,

Meredith knelt beside the boy until the mother returned with the blanket and started getting in her way again.

"Just tuck it around his arms and legs as much as you can," Meredith said between counting compressions. As soon as the mother finished that, she wanted to put the pillow under the boy's head, but Meredith got in the way, and the mother could not do anything.

The mother hugged the pillow to her chest while Meredith continued counting. Remembering that children need more rapid beats, Meredith sped her counting up. "One one-thousand, two one-thousand. I need someone to help me do this. Get me help." Meredith pleaded before she gave the boy the next breath. She looked around at the people as she did the compressions, and no one stepped forward.

Meredith's lungs were burning, and her legs from the knees down were numb from lack of circulation.

"One one-thousand, two one-thousand."

In the distance, sirens began their eerie chant along with Meredith's voice. She was never so glad to hear sirens in all her life. "Three one-thousand, four one-thousand."

The boy's chest heaved with a spasm and cough, but there was nothing after that. Meredith gave him a good breath and wondered what was taking the ambulance personnel so long to get out of their van.

Out of the corner of her eye, she could see it as she bent over the boy's face.

Then the attendant was standing next to her, and his mask was over the boy's face, and the rubber bag was gripped and released. The other attendant moved his hands over Meredith's, and she moved out of the way. She could not stand or even crawl; she just rolled away and sat there with her legs stretched out in front of her.

Lightheaded, dizzy, and unable to move with all the pins and needles in her legs, Meredith watched the scene continue in front of her. The men in the van did their job without too many words. The mother stood there hugging the pillow, and silent tears were rolling down her face. Once in a while she would wipe at her face. The silence of all the people was deafening. Soon, the attendants had the boy breathing on his own, and people started whispering to each other. Relief could be seen on faces, but no smiles.

The attendants put him in the van with his mother just two feet behind the stretcher.

The man in the blue checked shirt was standing next to Meredith, so she said, "Hey, thanks for helping me with the boy in the river."

"No problem," he replied.

"Come on, Bud," one of the guys standing next to him said.

Bud turned away from her and followed his friend. Other people started wandering away, but Meredith could not move. Her legs shook, and her chest still burned.

One of the attendants came out of the van and stepped over to Meredith. "You were the one to save the boy?"

Meredith nodded as the man picked up her wrist and checked her pulse.

"You also did all of the CPR?"

She nodded again as she watched him watch his watch.

"Your pulse is okay. How do you feel?"

"I'm okay. Just a bit shaky."

That seemed to satisfy him, and he quickly turned and got in the van but was back in just a minute with some orange juice for her. Almost immediately, he was back in the van, and it was gone. Alone, Meredith sat there and finished her juice, but could still not move without shaking.

People started walking slowly by and looked at her until she felt uncomfortable enough that she had to get up. Her feet wobbled at first, but she made them go one in front of the other until she was finally moving again. Returning to her tent, Meredith collapsed in an easy chair by the fire pit and watched as the neighbors got up from under their awning and went inside their camper.

Too tired to get up, Meredith sat there and stared at the unlit fire pit and the people as they walked past her campsite. Sometimes she felt that she was performing or on a platform because everyone would go by and stare; their heads turning like owls until they were out of eyesight. Meredith realized that she probably looked like a sight as she had run to save the boy, but it was worth it. She knew he was alive.

The man in the blue checked shirt walked by with his friends and laughingly said, "Hey, superwoman!"

Meredith replied, "Hey, Bud. "

"Who told you my name?" he demanded.

"Your friend said it when you were leaving before."

"Well, forget it, superwoman." They continued walking towards the park station.

Wishing she had a place somewhere more remote, Meredith decided to call it a day and get ready for bed early instead of sitting around the campsite. Tomorrow, memories would not be quite so clear, and people would not stare so much.

The tent was already hot, and Meredith felt sweaty when she awoke, so she headed to the showers before having breakfast. Some of the campers were moving around and Paige was already cooking breakfast for the guys in their camper. Meredith started her coffee in the little electric pot on top of the picnic table and started a fire in the pit.

That was one thing that her family always did when they were camping. Dad made the fire, and Meredith loved to get one of the sticks and poke around in the ashes and coals. One time they were camping and...

Some guys going by were laughing as they called out, "Hey, superwoman," interrupting Meredith's reminiscing. Recognizing Bud and his buddy, Meredith said nothing and continued staring at the fire. She had hoped for a nice, quiet weekend, but it looked like she should have stayed home and helped her husband with remodeling his mother's living room. He would have loved her in the way all the time! She smiled at the thought of that and started fussing around the campsite.

As she was fixing breakfast, the guys went back by and laughed and said, "Superwoman," under their breath.

Meredith thought about her mother and what her reaction would have been if they were her boys. But these were not boys. They were men who should have known better.

She thought they did this just because she was not pretty, and that made her angry. After eating breakfast, Meredith picked up her book to read but found it hard to concentrate, so she decided to take a walk around the park. Most of the people were out around their sites doing some cleaning or sitting in chairs. They nodded to her just like they did yesterday, but continued with what they were doing.

When she rounded the first corner of the campground, she stopped to look at the kids on the swings and then continued on down the drive toward the swimming hole. As she passed some of the campers, she could hear some laughing and heard, "Superwoman" again. Bud and his buddy were sitting at the picnic table and laughing. Their wives were doing dishes at the other end of the table, and a couple of children were playing on the grass. Meredith ignored them and tried to think of a way to stop this harassment.

After thinking about it, though, she realized they were not reacting to how she had looked when she had run down to the river, but they were reacting to her and what she had done. She knew they had no knowledge of first aid, so they might have thought what she had done was strange. Meredith decided to try an experiment and walked around the park a second time. This time, when she heard Bud say "Superwoman," she walked over to him.

Standing so that only he could hear, she said, "Constantly saying that makes you sound foolish. If you want to know how to save people's lives like that, stop by and I'll give you the secret to that power."

Without waiting for a response, she walked back over to the drive and continued finishing her walk. She felt much better after that and was able to sit down when she got back and pick up her book.

After a quiet day and afternoon, Meredith was working on some of her crafts at the table when Bud walked up.

"What did you mean when you said you could give me that kind of power?" he asked.

"It's not really power, Bud. It's more like knowledge."

"Oh, it's going back to school, huh?"

"Not really. There are adult classes that are only one day a week and easy to get into. Most schools provide these classes for free just because they want more people to learn first aid."

"Really? I might check that out," he said as he stood looking around. "Hey, sorry for giving you a hard time like that."

There was a bit of silence, and then he said, "What ya' got that can of lighter fluid there so close to the fire pit for? You trying wait for it to explode? Ya know they will when they get hot like that. You might have book smarts, but not common sense. I know what can happen with something like that. You better move that." He picked up the can and put it on the table. "What's this? Your matches on top of the can? You should know better than this!"

"You're absolutely right, Bud. I must not have common sense because I knew that I shouldn't put that can there, and especially not with the matches on top."

Meredith got up and put the matches back in the plastic container and said, "Bud, I may know how to fix people up once they are hurt, but I think you have the best idea."

"What's that?"

"Don't mess up in the first place!" They both started laughing.

# Dare to Hope

Jason saw his brother sitting on the porch. Even with all the determination he had before, Jason was still afraid to show Tim the book. Looking down at his feet, Jason shuffled over to Tim and sat down. Jason held the book in his hands and slid it between his knees.

"Whatcha' got?" Tim asked in sign language.

Mouthing a silent prayer, Jason lifted the book and held it tightly in his hands.

"Another book. S'pose you want me to read it to you." Without him thinking about it, Tim's hands moved swiftly. He never noticed his hands. Even the dirty nails were ignored.

Silent as always, Jason looked up with his blue eyes showing fear, and he shook his head. Still holding tightly to the book, Jason held it out to his brother. Unlike Tim, Jason's fingers were clean, and the nails were filed short.

"If ya don't want me to read it to ya, whatcha' want me to do with it?" Tim always read Jason's books to him, even though Jason could read for himself. This started before Jason learned to read for himself. Now, Tim didn't read as often, but Jason still came with books.

Jason pointed shyly to Tim and gave the book to him.

Tim's dirty face held a puzzled look at his brother. "Do you want me to keep this book?" he signed.

Jason shook his head and signed back, "You read for yourself."

Tim picked up the book and began reading using sign language as well as saying the words from habit.

"Escape." Tim turned a few pages and continued, "Chapter one. The cold air hit me as I ran out of the trailer. It was still better to be out in the cold rather than to listen to that. Dad must be high on something again. This time it was Paul who got it and not me. I ran over to the playground across the street and sat on the swing. At least here I couldn't hear what was happening inside the house.

I knew what Paul was going through. *It's not fair!* I thought as I kicked the swing into motion. The other kids in here don't live like this. Their fathers don't beat them! Besides that, they had better houses. Our mobile home was the smallest in the park. Some of the kids in the park even had their own bedroom.

I could see Scott, three trailers away from us., peek out of his bedroom window. He was one of the lucky ones. He had his own bedroom. It's not fair! I pumped harder. I could feel the swing going so high that it jumped every time it reached the height of the bars. Up... jump, kick, that one was to dad for hitting Paul; down... up... jump, kick, that one was for hitting me; down... up... jump, kick, that one was for hitting Ma! One of these days, I'm going to go right over that bar, right up to the sky, and fly like a bird. Get away from here.

I heard a door slam, so I stopped pumping to see what was going on. Scott's trailer was closer to the swings, and I could see him as he jumped down the steps, both feet landing at the same time on each step; then he ran over to the swings.

"Hi ya, Pete! Whatca' doin'?"

"What's it look like? I'm swingin'." I started pumping harder, getting back up to the jump.

"You mad at me or somethin'?"

37

"Nah," I answered as I started to let the swing slow down. "You wanna go by Mrs. Frost's?" I leaned back in the swing to let the funny feeling go into my stomach as the swing came down and up.

"Un, unh. We get in trouble every time we go there." Scott just kind of sat there on the swing, not getting his feet off the ground, but moving back and forth.

The squeak of the swings was the only sound we made for a while. Scott was a nice kid, but he always wore better clothes than ours. At least they didn't have holes in them. I started pumping as hard as I could. It would be neat to fly away.

Up... jump... kick... down. Up... jump... kick... down. Concentrating on getting as high as I could, Scott's voice broke my thoughts. "Pete! Chain's gonna' break." Up... jump... kick... down...

"Pete! Hey, Pete!"

"What?" I heard him as if he was miles away. I wished I was miles away.

Maybe I could walk somewhere. Where would I go?

"Where's your dad going?" Scott asked as the rusted Plymouth Satellite drove past us. Scott's swing was stopped, and he had his arms wrapped around the chains so they tucked into the inside of his elbows.

I slowed down to see what was going on. "Dunno. He's not going towards town. Let's go to my house and see."

Slowing the swing, I jumped off before it stopped. That was one of the many reasons why I had holes in my tennis shoes all the time. Anxious to see what happened to Paul, I ran over to the trailer. I wanted to talk Ma into getting out of here. Usually, parents don't listen to a twelve-year-old, though. Most of the time, dad just hit us, but he was pretty crazy today. As I opened the trailer door, the heat hit me in a blast. The TV in the corner blared out, "What's up, Doc?" Bugs Bunny was looking at a gun, his whiskers wrinkling up as he munched on a carrot.

"All right!" Scott ran over to the set and plopped on the floor. "My favorite." He peeled his jersey off, leaving the sleeves inside out. It was weird that at 14 he was older than me, but still liked cartoons.

Leaving him sitting on the floor, I followed the muffled sounds coming from the back of the trailer, and broken dishes crunched as I went through the kitchen. Other dirty dishes were still in the sink of cold water. Once I got through the kitchen, I could hear Mom's voice and Paul's muffled sobs.

"Dad didn't mean to hurt you. You know that."

"Liar! Liar!" I said as I stood in the doorway of the bedroom. Mom was sitting on the bed next to Paul and holding a cold cloth to his face. Usually, Dad didn't hit us there. I'm probably going to get blamed for that one. We never said, "Dad did it." Paul looked up at me. Tears still tracked down his face, smearing the dirt and leaving a dark smudge on his left cheek; his right was hidden behind the bloodstained washcloth.

I said, "Mom, he meant it, and you know it."

"Hush, now; don't make your brother cry anymore." She had one hand around Paul's shoulder, and the other held the washcloth in place. Her blue jeans were ripped in the knees, and the lettering on her sweatshirt was faded and barely readable.

"It's not my fault he's hurt. You can't blame it on me." Paul had stopped crying, so I continued, "Besides that, you've got to say something at school Monday, and I didn't do it!"

"Okay, okay; we'll talk about it later."

Mom handed me the washcloth and said, "Go get me a band-aid. It's only a scratch and one should cover it."

I took the washcloth to the bathroom, rinsed it out, and retrieved the band-aid and ointment. A cockroach scuttled out of the way as I shut the cabinet door. "I hate this place!" I mumbled and went back to the bedroom. "Where did Dad go?" I asked Mom.

"I don't know." She wiped off Paul's face and made sure the bleeding wouldn't come through the band-aid.

"Let's get out of here before he comes back. I want to get away before something worse happens," I said.

"I don't have the car. Besides, he'll be fine when he comes home. This won't happen again."

"Yeah, but what about next time? You know he's gonna get high again. Just like you promised then."

"Pete, Dad's just upset. We'll be okay."

"No, we won't! Other kids don't live this way; why do we have to?" I shouted.

I'll see what we can do tomorrow, okay?" She stopped picking up the toys.

"Like what?" I wanted to know if she really meant that she would try to get away from him. Paul looked better now, and he started helping her pick up toys.

"I'll talk to Dad; maybe we can make him see what's happening. He wasn't this way when he was working. Once he gets a job, things will get better; you watch and see. Now go on an' play, the both of you." She had never made promises like this before. She looked sad. It must be hard for her, too.

I went back to the living room. Scott was still watching the cartoons, but Mario replaced Bugs Bunny on the screen. The house seemed too warm to me. I felt like I was suffocating. I knew that if I didn't get out, an asthma attack would start up soon.

"What's goin' on?" Scott said to the screen in front of him.

"Nuthin'. Let's get outta' here." I flicked the TV off and headed to the door. Scott usually followed me anywhere I went, so I didn't even look to see if he was coming.

Pulling the sleeves of his jersey, Scott followed behind me as I stepped out on the porch. I ran down the steps, to the road, past the other mobile homes, and didn't stop until we were past Scott's house.

"Slow up!" he called to me. "What's goin' on?" He finished zipping up his jersey and caught up to me.

"Nuthin'." I shivered and thought I should have grabbed a jacket for myself, but I hated wearing it; everything around our place was torn.

"Hey, if you don't want me aroun' just say so."

"Nah, it's not that. Dad's been messin' with us; that's all. Let's go over to Mrs. Frost's."

"Un, Unh; why do you always want to go over there and ruin her flowers?" Scott shoved his hands in his pocket as we slowed down.

"Cause I feel like it."

"Let's go by the office, instead, and see if we can get the video games to work. "

We never had money to play the games, but every now and then we could get one of the machines to give us a game or two, so we headed there.

Since there were no sidewalks in our trailer park, we walked down the road to the office. I was sure the cat saw us before we saw it, but it didn't move. As we got closer to it, I noticed that its orange and white coat was matted with burrs, and part of its fur was missing. "Hey! Look at that!" I exclaimed as I pointed to the cat.

"Wonder where it came from?"

"I don't know; never seen it before."

Sure that it would run away, I started running toward it. Its amber eyes watched me come up, but it didn't move. Then I kicked at it. When I did, I slipped and fell, missing the cat. It still didn't move. "What kind of cat are you anyway?" I picked up a stone and threw it, but missed again.

Scott laughed, "Maybe you should take up ballet or somthin' to learn to walk." Still laughing, he ran toward the cat, but stopped when he got near me. Holding out his hand, Scott helped me get up from the ground. The cat still stood there watching us. Its tail twitched back and forth. "Aw, come on Pete; leave the cat go."

"It's a weird creature. It don't look right. Maybe we should tell the office about it," I said.

"Un, Unh; leave it be."

Giving it some distance, I walked past it and brushed off my ripped jeans. Mom wouldn't even notice one more tear in my play clothes. We went over to the video room, which was a rectangular room off the office and had arcade games in it. Scott always went to the race car one, and I went to "Dungeons and Dragons."

There were eight machines in all, but not that many kids played them except on the weekends, and then the room was always full with the older kids. The poured cement floor and cement block walls were a dingy gray-green color that looked like someone had taken many different colors and put them all together. One window on the wall by the door had paint that had dropped on the pane and left a gray streak. We tried to coax the machines to give us a free game, but they were more stubborn than I was. Giving one of the machines a kick, I turned around to look out the window. Inside the room and on the sill, the cat was sitting and watching everything we did.

That cat was strange. It just sat there watching us. Its eyes were half closed because the light from the window was shining right on it.

"Scott," I called. "Look, the cat's on the sill."

"Man, leave it alone. It just wants to get warm. Let's get outa' here."

"Okay," I said. This was the first time Scott ever suggested anything. We might as well go home. It was getting late anyway.

Tim stopped reading from the book and looked at Jason. Silent tears brought back more memories than Tim wanted to feel. Before his voice choked, Tim started reading again.

Tim's voice was still a bit shaky, but he ignored that. "Dad didn't come home the whole weekend, and Mom was acting kind of funny, saying things about people we hadn't heard about before, all of her sisters, and how nice they were. We met one when she came to our house with Grandma a long time ago, and all I could remember about her was that she was big and didn't let us do very much.

Then came the day.

I got off the school bus and could see his car from the window of the bus. Even with the sound of the bus pulling away, I could hear their voices from the driveway. Mom was saying something really loud, and Dad was yelling back at her. I didn't want to go in there. Since Mom always made us change our clothes before we went out to play, as quietly as I could, I opened the door and slipped into my bedroom. They were in their room talking about someone from the school. Now I knew why Paul wasn't on the bus. They must have brought him home.

I changed my clothes and threw them on the bed like Mom always wanted us to. Then I peeked out the door to see if they were looking toward my room. No one in sight, but I could hear them.

"What'd you tell them that for?" Dad yelled.

"What did you expect me to tell them? That you hit him?"

I couldn't believe that she said that to him. Usually, she didn't talk back to Dad, and she sounded scared. I knew I was! I didn't want them to hear me, so I inched toward the living room.

"Whattheyplanondoinnow?" Dad's words slid together as if they were all one word and muffled by his hands.

"I don't know." Mom's voice was quiet and shaky, but she continued, "The school phoned me to come and get him this morning, so Julie and I went over there and picked him up."

Just as I got to the front door, I could hear something breaking. I knew he was going to hurt Mom, but what could I do? Slipping out the front, I started running to the office. Then I heard a door slam and our car start up. It went the other way, and I couldn't see who was in it. Afraid it was Dad still in the trailer, I went to the swings instead of the office and watched the trailer with intent eyes. Small tornadoes of leaves whirled in the road, revealing gusts of wind that usually remain hidden. A flock of birds flew over, honking at each other. Afraid of missing something, I didn't swing like I usually did. Nothing happened.

Scott came out of his trailer, and we started to play around the park. The cat wasn't in the video room when we went in, but when we left, it was there. I didn't see it until I stubbed my toe trying to get one of the machines working. The cat's amber eyes flashed warnings at me until we finally left. Then we hung around Scott's place the rest of the day. The day seemed to take a long time to go by. Most days, supper came before I was ready for it. I watched for the car, but it never did show up. Finally, we went to the park and sat on the swings for a while. I was surprised when two cars and a U-Haul truck pulled in front of my house. I hopped off the swings and ran over to them as Mom got out of one of the cars.

"Hi," I said.

"Pete, don't ask any questions, just do as I say. Go with Aunt Karen and stay with her. I'll be with you in just a little while." She grabbed my arm and shoved me into one of the cars.

"Where's Paul?" I asked her, but Mom had the door closed before I could hear what she said next. I turned to Aunt Karen. She looked nice but determined. I was afraid but hopeful. "Is Mom coming?

Aunt Karen was already driving out of the park's driveway. The cat was walking down the road going south. He looked in better condition, as if someone had given him a new coat.

"We're going to see your brother; your mom will be coming later," Aunt Karen said. "By the way, my name is..."

"I know," I interrupted. "It's Aunt Karen; Mom's been telling us about you and Aunt Julie. Where we goin?"

"To Aunt Julie's house. Have you ever been there?"

"No," I replied, "We just came from Texas."

"Please put your seat belt on." Aunt Karen's voice was firm but gentle. I put the seat belt on as we pulled onto the expressway. "Your brother's at Aunt Julie's house. We'll go there to wait for your mom."

"What's going to happen after that?" I looked around at the car. It was a fairly new model Oldsmobile, and smelled clean. Not new, clean, but cleanser clean.

My mind was racing. I thought, are we finally getting out of there? I was too afraid to ask the question, but it was there, though. I wanted her to tell me what was going to happen, and that everything was going to be alright. The radio was low and playing what the announcer called "easy listening" music, the kind that I heard when I went into the doctor's office. I hated going, but went there a lot for my asthma. Just thinking about it made my breathing faster. She was saying something, what was it?

"...not sure what will happen after that." She kept looking at the road and the mirrors a lot.

"How long are we going to be on the expressway?"

"Not much farther now. It won't take long." She was not a pretty woman, I thought. She was short and fat like Mrs. Frost but not as big as Aunt Julie. Her sweater was a new greenish color that matched her pants. Everything was loose-fitting. She had pretty hair, though; all curled in back and short on the sides.

"Is it okay if I sing?" I asked. "Singing helps me get my mind off asthma."

"Sure."

I started singing, "Deep and wide, deep and wide, there's a fountain flowing deep and wide..." I was surprised when she started singing with me. Her voice wasn't the greatest, but she sang quietly, which made me feel like she was a nice person. Before I knew it, we were off the expressway and into town. We drove for only a short way, and Aunt Karen was quiet while I sang. We pulled into a driveway by a small house that had paint peeling off it.

Paul came running out of the house next door. I was never so glad to see him in all my life. I got the door open and tried to get out, but then I had to unsnap the seat belt. My legs couldn't move fast enough!

Paul grabbed my arm and said, "Isn't this neat? Look over here." We took off behind the house. There was a boat on a trailer in the backyard next to the garage.

After she talked to the neighbor, Aunt Karen called us over to the house before we could get into the boat, so we went in the back door. This place didn't smell as clean as the car. There were things like boots, bleach, and potatoes scattered on the steps going up to the kitchen from the back door. The kitchen was small without a table in it, and the table was in the next room which was also part of the living room.

"Are you boys hungry?" Aunt Karen opened the refrigerator door.

"Ya!" We both yelled out.

I walked over to the basement stairs by the back door to see where they went and discovered a rifle leaning against the wall in the corner of the stairs. "Paul! Come here! Look what I found!" I was going to pull it up to my shoulder when Aunt Karen came to the top of the steps.

"Put that thing down!" she exclaimed! "I don't want to catch you playing with that thing at all. It's not a toy, it's not yours, and they are dangerous. You have to wait until Uncle John can show them to you."

"Who is Uncle John?" Not waiting for an answer, I continued, "Do you live here?"

"No, I don't, and Uncle John is Aunt Julie's husband. They'll bring your mother here in a little while, so that you can talk to him about the gun another time. I also don't want you to go downstairs until they get here."

"Okay," I said disappointingly. While Aunt Karen worked in the kitchen, Paul and I went into the living room and started looking around the house. There were two bedrooms. In the one that looked like a storage room, the bed was made. It had a computer on a desk that filled the corner.

The other bedroom was all messy; the bed hadn't been made, and things were strewn all over the place. Then we found it.

"What's in this brown zipped-up bag under the bed?" Paul asked.

"Let's see!" I grabbed the bag, which was as tall as Paul, and lifted it onto the bed. It was heavy, but I easily lifted it and had it half zipped open when Aunt Karen came in the door. How she knew we had it, I'll never know. It was like she had eyes all over the house.

Grabbing the bag's handle, Aunt Karen said, "Guns are very dangerous and not something to be playing with. I know neither one of you would like it if your brother accidentally hurt you when you were looking at it. I think we'll leave this room off limits also." She pointed to the door, and we were done exploring in there.

We ended up going to Micky D'S and brought the food back to the house to eat.

We started making hats out of newspaper and someone pulled in the driveway. Aunt Karen looked out and said, "Your mother is here."

We were out the door in a flash. The U-Haul was in the backyard behind the house. Grandma was even there!

"Boys, we need to have a talk," Mom said. "Let's go inside and sit down."

All the way in the house we had questions for her, "What's going on? Are we going back home?" but she didn't say anything until we got inside and sat down between us on the couch. Then she started to explain.

"You know how hard it's been for us at home? Well, I've decided to get us out of there before one of us gets hurt bad."

She touched Paul's face where he had the black eye and the sore on his cheek. "We're going to be staying here and at grandma's house until we can find a place of our own."

A thousand questions were racing through my mind. I couldn't pay attention to all she was saying, but yet I heard everything she said, plus I heard the clock ticking on the wall, and Aunt Karen and Aunt Julie bringing things in from the U-Haul. The noise from the street seemed to demand more attention than before.

"You're not going to the same schools, so we'll have to make arrangements there. I don't want you boys to go with anyone unless I tell you it's okay. Especially not your father. He may make all kinds of promises to you, but don't listen to them. If you see him down the street, you come and get me. Is that clear?"

Not going to the same schools? Not having the same friends? That would be okay with me, but Paul looked scared. He was only 10, and I remembered how the kids in the Texas schools picked on him. I hoped it wouldn't happen again. It was bad enough having Dad hurt us, but that wasn't going to happen anymore! No more fighting! Ya Hoo!

Mom got up from the couch as she was saying, "...So now let's go help Aunt Karen and Aunt Julie. "

Paul and I ran out the back door to the U-Haul and there stood a great big man with a bushy black beard! We stopped dead in our tracks and Mom said, "Boys, this is Uncle John, he will help you get things out of the truck, and you can take them into the house and put them in the living room. Uncle John, this is Pete and this one is Paul."

"Hi, boys! It's nice to finally meet you!" Uncle John grabbed a bag from the truck and held it out towards us. "Here ya go! Time to get to work!"

Darkness had set in, and the street lights had come on, which started casting shadows on the bushes in the back yard. I was never scared of the dark like I was of Dad. Uncle John seemed like a very nice man, even though he looked like Grizzly Adams! Since Aunt Julie screamed every time she saw a cockroach and Uncle John had to go where she was and kill it, he decided to leave the rest of the stuff in the truck and throw some bug bombs in there.

Uncle John climbed into the back of the truck to throw a bomb in the very back. As he stepped toward the middle of the truck, we heard an animal screech, and Uncle John fell backward. The orange cat from the trailer park jumped on top of Uncle John, then bounded out of the truck, and landed by Paul.

"You crazy cat!" I couldn't believe that it had gotten into our truck and come all the way here. "Get outa' here!"

I started to run and kick at it at the same time. Its eyes blazed red, and it moved. When I turned to see where the cat went, Paul was sitting on the ground holding his leg. I had missed the cat and had kicked Paul instead!

"Paul, you okay?" Bending down beside him, I could see the hurt in his face. It was like the looks he gave Dad when he got crazy.

"I'm sorry, Paul. I didn't mean to hurt you."

"Why did you want to hurt the cat?" He asked as he started getting up. The cat still stood there, its tail twitching.

"I dunno." The fear he had for Dad was still on his face. I didn't want to be like Dad! But that is just what I was doing! "Paul, I know this sounds just like Dad, but I won't do anything like that again. Honest, I won't. Help me remember that, okay?" I held my hand out to help him up.

Paul looked at me. "Okay." His eyes were big, the whites showing like mirrors of the street lamps that glared from behind the house. I gave him a hug and we stood up. He looked better. I never wanted anyone to look at me like that again.

Uncle John finally got himself up and out of the back of the truck. "What was that?"

"Just a stray cat we've been seeing around the park. Do you think we can keep it?" I asked as I bent down by it.

"Neither of you boys was there, so how did you put it in the truck?" Uncle John looked at the cat.

It was sitting next to me and let me put my hand on it. Why it hadn't run away after all I had done to it, I didn't know, but it sat there without moving.

"You'll have to ask your mother... No, even if she doesn't want to keep it, it can stay here if it wants to."

I was not surprised as the cat closed its eyes and began to purr.

It wasn't long after we moved out that Mom told us how good Dad was doing in his new job, and how he had changed for the better. The End"

Tim finished reading and looked at his brother. Jason was still crying silent tears that rolled down into the corners of his mouth.

"You afraid of me?" Tim signed.

Jason shook his head and signed back, "Can we get out, too?"

Tim put a hand on Jason's shoulder. The shirt wasn't new, but unlike Tim's, it was clean. Then he looked up at the house as if it were a mountain to climb. Taking Jason's hand, Tim signed, "Let's go talk to Dad."

Together they went inside the house to the kitchen where their father was reading the paper. With hope in their hearts, they handed their father Escape.

# Second Place Success

Grabbing last-minute items for the journey, Wendy loaded her arms as full as she could and carried the bags down the stairs to the brown Chevette in the parking lot. Then she double-checked her purse. It was time to hit the highway, so she started the car and glanced at the dashboard clock: 7:30 PM.

"Not bad," she thought. She had loaded the car in one hour after working eight hours. Anxious to get going, she moved the car through traffic quickly. Now, all she had to do was drive for the next twelve to fourteen hours.

In the first five hours, the traffic on the expressway was mild. Occasionally, she wound around a car in the fast lane that should have been in the slow lane, but most of the time hers was the only set of headlights on the road. Keeping the car moving as fast as she dared above the speed limit, and because she treated her car well, it performed well for Wendy as she pulled onto the Ohio turnpike.

Headlights glared from both the rear-view mirrors and made her tighten her grip on the steering wheel. Noticing the heater throwing hotter air after getting on the turnpike, she kept herself in the slow lane while trucks zoomed past her in the fast lane. Glancing at the gauges on the dash, she realized that not only was her engine getting warm, but she was also getting tired enough for a break.

"Should have stopped for a break before getting on the turnpike," she grumbled to herself.

Thinking of a nice long vacation, Wendy eased her foot on the gas pedal and allowed her muscles to relax a little, but her mind kept jumping to the job she had just quit. "Nurses should be paid more than what he offered, and he didn't even offer a vacation. Now he will have to find another employee," she thought. "But I'll never know what success is."

There was a better-paying nursing job waiting for her in two weeks, and she hoped this boss would be better than the last one. "Just because he had more clout than the one who hired her, he thought he could make me lose vacation time coming to me," she grumbled. "I'll go see the other boss when I get back." Her hands tightened on the wheel with determination.

The cold plastic of the wheel brought her attention back to the road, and she realized that the huge trucks all around her were buffeting her little Chevette all around.

She hated being boxed in. The truck in front of her was slowing down, and the sticker "How's my driving?" laughed at her impatience. The headlights of the truck behind her seemed bigger and brighter now. The truck to her left was creeping up almost to her rear bumper. The edge of the turnpike was on her right.

"I have to get out of here," she thought. "Come on, Bessie; show me your stuff." Pushing the gas pedal down, she scooted the front of her car closer to the truck in front of her and quickly pulled the brown Chevette toward the truck to her left. Creating a door in the traffic, she slid out of the truckers' grasp and into the darkness of the fast lane. With their horns blowing a salute, the truckers let her continue unimpeded in the fast lane.

"Were there only those few trucks on the road? Why were they boxing me in like that? It's time to take a break and get off this trap, but where?" she thought.

The first exit off the turnpike after that was just a rest area with too many trucks there, so Wendy passed a few others until she found one that would get her off the turnpike completely. Pulling her car into the parking lot of a restaurant, she glanced at the dashboard clock: 3 AM. After parking her car in a spot close to the restaurant's door, she finally relaxed her shoulders and shut the engine down.

The restaurant's door pulled open easily, and Wendy walked up to the counter.

There was just one man behind the counter and no other customers in the coffee house.

"A large black coffee, please."

"For here or to go?" he asked as he wiped his hands on his dirty apron.

"For here."

As she waited for her coffee, she looked for a seat that would give her a clear view of her car. She took the coffee from him and turned toward the empty tables and booths. As she slid into her seat, the door of the restaurant opened, and two men walked in and up to the counter. Pulling maps out of her purse, she began looking at the one showing the turnpike.

In the background, she heard, "Hi Joe, Tom. Haven't seen you in two weeks; where ya been?" the man behind the counter called.

"On the road out east of here. Give us the usual," said the man in the faded blue denim jacket, walking up to the counter, while the other one in the red plaid, quilted jacket turned and leaned against the counter.

Blue jacket kept talking to the man behind the counter, and red jacket kept leaning against the counter with his back to them. He looked around the room and looked at the girl in the booth. She quickly looked out the window again to make sure all was quiet around her car.

Red jacket walked over to her booth, and the two men at the counter became very quiet. "That your car out there?"

"You mean the brown Chevette?" She quickly picked up the maps and started putting them back in her purse.

"Ain't no other car out there is there?" he said.

"Yes, it is." She started sliding out of her booth. "I needed to stop and get myself a coffee..."

"Hey, wait a minute, lady. Don't go gettin all riled up now. Everything is alright with yer car. No one is moving around it. We jes saw you on the pike en had to say that was one of the first times someone has gotten out'en a box on us before. No, no, you don't need to get up. Finnish yer coffee. Yer hood's plenty hot and could stand some coolin." Red jacket paused as blue jacket came up.

Blue jacket said, "Don't worry; everything is fine. Just sit and finish your coffee."

Without ice water to steal from, she sipped her steaming hot coffee as quickly as possible. The three men were sitting on the opposite side of the room, and she knew they were talking about how they boxed her in. Fearing they would plan something else, she quickly gulped another mouth full of hot coffee and left the dregs. She didn't bother to leave a tip, but grabbed her purse and walked out the door.

As she went past her car, Wendy's hand slid across the hood, and she could feel the heat of the engine, but it wasn't so hot that she couldn't put her hand all the way down; she would still have to slow down. The road was dark and quiet, and she was left with her thoughts. Since she was halfway there, everything would be okay. Steve would have planned a nice, relaxing vacation for her.

It was noon by the time Wendy was able to stop and telephone Steve to say that she was in town. He told her to wait and met her at the phone booth. He showed her where the motel was, and she could finally get some rest. He promised to return after he got out of work at 5 PM. That left her with just a short nap after being up for over 24 hours.

Promptly, he arrived at 5:30. "There's a car race tonight about twenty miles from here; think you'd like to go?" Standing there in his uniform, he looked very dignified, not what would be expected at a race track.

He was trying very hard to be nice, but going to a race track sounded like the last place she wanted to be. "That sounds like fun," Wendy lied.

"Well, I kinda expected you'd like to go, so I made arrangements. You don't mind?"

"No." She really was having second thoughts about this vacation and wanted to forget about the race, but she was afraid that if she said anything, he would cut the visit short, and she really did like him. "What kind of races?"

"There will be 2 races run and even a power puff derby..." his voice trailed on as they walked to her car. He was still talking about the races as they drove out of town. "You've never been to a race track before, have you?"

"No, there was one on the highway about 10 miles from our house, but I never went to..."

"Well, you're in for a surprise and a treat. I know how you like to drive, and these people know how to drive..." his chatter filled the dead space in her Chevette with empty praise.

Why did she allow these things to happen? "Do you remember Terry and Dori?" she asked.

"Boy, I haven't seen Terry in a long time. What's he been up to?" The small talk floated in the Chevette, and long, silent spaces began building wedges. By the time they made it to the track, they both felt relieved. He pulled the car off the highway and into the haze surrounding the track. A cloud of dirt surrounded the track, its sign, circled around them, and was in the car before they reached a parking spot. Each footstep she took seemed heavier than the last. People were lined up in front of the gates until they got their tickets, and then they were herded through the gates.

"I know what it's like the first time at a place like this, so do you want something to drink before we go up in the bleachers?" Steve shouted over the noise of the crowd and cars.

"I know what you mean, and it does sound good." The colas, in red and white wax cups, were watered down and had little ice to cut the grit in the air. Wendy repeatedly chastised herself for agreeing to come as they worked their way halfway up the bleachers.

"It's best to sit up here so that you can see the whole track. The last time I came, they had some pretty good races. Most of the locals..." his voice was drowned out by the deafening sound of engines coming closer, and she could tell he was enjoying the atmosphere. The people on the bleachers were debating who was going to be racing and who would be winning. The air around them became more electric as time went on. Steve explained as much as he could about the track and other tracks and races he had been to. After a while, even he admitted that it was taking too long for the races to start.

The crowd in the stands grew more and more restless as the cars remained unlined. The scene below looked like the freeze frame was turned on and left there, waiting for someone to activate the remote.

"I'm going down there to see what's going on." Steve said, "Do you want to go with me?"

"No, there are too many people down there; I'll wait here." Wendy sat there and watched him work his way down through the crowd. Several others were coming back up to the bleachers and talking about what should be going on, but wasn't. Bits and pieces of the conversations floated through the air, and in spite of herself, she was curious.

Steve had been gone just a short while, and then she could see him working his way back up through the crowd. Swinging himself around and sitting next to her, he explained, "They're missing only one woman driver to complete the quota needed for the 'powder-puff' derby, but they can't find one more driver so they can start the races. They are holding it for only a few more minutes, and then they will start the regular races. I wish they would have the 'powder-puff' because I haven't seen it done here. I've seen it done on other tracks, but not here."

"Is there something special about this track?" Wendy asked.

"This is one of the biggest tracks in this state, and it's bigger than all the other places I've been to."

"How big are they usually?"

Most are a quarter of a mile, and this is half a mile, but I mean this is one of the more prominent or famous ones. Boy, I wish they would find someone to drive."

"All the person has to do is drive around the track?"

"Yup."

"Do they have to have a special license?" Wendy asked.

"Nuh uh, even you could go down there and race. Hey, you wouldn't want to, would you? You're a good driver! Come on!"

"I don't know, Steve. I've never even seen a race before except on TV, and then I watched for only a few minutes. They'll find someone else, watch and see."

"Let's go down there anyway, maybe they won't," Steve said. "Besides, I'd be able to brag about you then."

Grabbing her hand, Steve pulled her up, and they began working their way to the pits. The smell of sweat became stronger as they worked their way closer. It mingled with oil and gasoline and almost made her gag, but she ignored the feeling as she listened to the women chatting.

"We've got to find just one more to drive," a woman in a plaid shirt said to a man standing in the pits and holding a clipboard.

"We haven't had a good run in months. Even if we don't find someone to drive, let us have this race light."

"You know I can't do that," he replied, "and we have to get the guys' cars lined up pretty soon."

"Excuse me," Steve interrupted. "Here's someone who can drive."

"Boy, it takes more than someone who can drive. Some of those women out there drive worse than men. She has to be able to race."

"I know that she is a good driver; give her a chance," Steve countered.

The woman in plaid interjected, "Don't look a gift horse in the mouth. Let her drive no matter what, so we can have our race!" She started shoving the others to their cars and said, "Let's get this thing started!

"Have you ever driven in a race before?" the clipboard man asked.

"No," Wendy answered.

"I don't know about this. Hold on, Sally."

"Hey, com'on!" Sally, in the plaid top, responded and stopped to turn to Wendy. "Give us a chance. Are you a good driver?" she asked Wendy.

"I think so!" Wendy shouted over the sudden roaring of engines.

"You have to do more than think so. To be out here, you have to know so!" Sally said.

"I know so! I just came thirteen hundred miles by myself without any trouble, so I feel I am a good driver," Wendy shouted.

Sally said to the clipboard man, "Let's do this!"

"I need to see your driver's license," the clipboard man said to Wendy.

"What car will she drive?" Sally asked.

"I can't drive my own car," Wendy answered. "It's too small and it's only a four-cylinder."

A man in a gray suit, who had been standing behind Sally, said, "You can use mine. Can you drive a stick?"

"That's what mine is anyway, but I would like to have a chance to go around the track before the race," Wendy said.

"That's not fair!" One of the remaining women complained.

"I think it is fair because I have never been on this or any other race track before," Wendy said. "Have all of you raced on this track before?

"All of us have," Sally said. "It would only be fair to let her do it. Com'on! Let's get started!" Sally herded the rest to their cars while the gray-suited man helped get his car ready for the race.

Steve tapped Wendy on her back and said, "I know you can beat all of them! Have a good time out there!"

They walked out to the car that was set up for Wendy, and the two of them looked it over. There was no glass in the side or back windows, and there was an extra roll bar bracing the center of the roof of the car.

Having been stripped of all of its trappings except its silver finish, the make of the car was hard to discern. Wendy went to open the door, but she found it welded shut. Looking up to ask Steve about it, she noticed the other drivers climbing in the windows of their cars, so she looked at how high the window was and thought how short her legs were.

"Damn, how do I get myself into these messes?" she thought.

Sally approached and halted her before she could begin climbing in.

"Here, put this on." Sally handed her a helmet and started laughing, "You can't even get in there with your short legs!" Hooking up the helmet, Sally looked at her, "You're not familiar with races, are you? At first, I was worried about you beating me, but I don't think I have too much to worry about. I think I'll concentrate on a couple of the others, but I think I have this race already won. Here, let me help you. There is a grab hold right up here..."

Steve was already helping Wendy get in and gave her a good luck hug and kiss. "See you at the finish!" he yelled, but the helmet made his voice sound distant and funny.

Because the engine was already running, Wendy looked at the dashboard to see what was there. Like the outside, she discovered much had been stripped. Hooking the seat belt in, she took the car out of gear and put it through its paces. The power of the engine could be felt right away. She was not used to so much power, and she wondered if she should discover how fast this machine could go. Deciding against flooring it, she paced herself to the far turn and noticed the gravel on the outside of the turn. "I have to remember that is there when we get to this spot," she thought.

Wendy finished her run around the track and pulled up to the end of the line of other cars. Gray coat poked his head in the window and said, "You'll have to do better than that to win this race; don't embarrass this car, and don't scratch her! Get in line over there," he pointed to a spot almost in the middle of the pack of cars and hit the side of the car to signal for her to move.

Once she was in place, Wendy sat there and noticed her senses becoming more acute. Her ears felt like how a dog's ears look when they are curious, her back muscles were tight and tense, so she moved her hands to the bottom of the steering wheel like her father taught her to do when they were on long trips and needed to relax. Her eyes scanned the drivers around her. Her ears heard nothing but the ringing in her own ears that she always noticed when it was very quiet. It was not quiet now! The engines were revving up!

"How am I to know when to move? Where am I supposed to park when I get done? How did I get myself in this mess?" Wendy thought to herself. Then the cars started moving slowly. "I didn't hear a gun go off. How did they know to move?" She wondered again. Keeping her hands at the bottom of the steering wheel, she shifted her weight to her side to be more relaxed. "These cars are not moving very fast. I need to get up further so I can get passed the slow ones."

Again, Wendy scanned the drivers around her. They appeared frightened, hands positioned at two and ten, faces taut, and shoulders hunched forward. She turned her left signal on since there was a hole in the line there; before the car behind her could close the gap, she had moved her car into the small space and was getting to the inside lane where she wanted to be to avoid the gravel in the turn. Closing the distance between her and the car in front of her was easy. Pulling back into her own lane let her pass this car and get in front of the two she had passed. She pulled into the inside lane again and passed the one in second place. Now she was coming up to the leader.

The leader, Sally, looked at her with a surprised face, but then she mocked Wendy and put her hands on the bottom of the steering wheel.

"I'm in second place; let's see what this baby can do!" Demanding performance rather than controlling performance, she pushed the gas pedal as far as it would go and pulled into first place. Sally didn't like that at all, so she sped her car up even with Wendy. Time seemed to stand still in the front stretch. They stayed even with each other until they came to the end of it.

Because they were nearing the turn and she wanted to avoid the gravel on the outside, Wendy slowed just enough to maintain control while in the turn. Sally, however, kept her speed up and strayed into the outside lane. They entered the turn with Sally in the outside lane and lost control.

Not wanting Sally to hit his car, Wendy floored it and pulled the car tighter into the inside lane, giving Sally more room; once there, Wendy had to reduce her speed fractionally to maintain control throughout the turn. Sally kept her speed but had trouble maintaining control in the turn. Once the turn was done, Sally pulled back into first, but not by much. The two stayed that way for the rest of the back stretch, but Sally came in first place.

The race was over. Wendy still did not know where to park the car, so she sat back and relaxed her muscles. Her car slowly rounded the turn after the finish line, and Sally's car disappeared out of her line of vision in the rear-view mirror. "I'll just go around the track again and park wherever I see others park," Wendy thought.

Her muscles continued to relax as she started around the track the second time, but she felt uncomfortable as she pulled up behind the slower cars still on the track at the back turn. After passing a couple of more cars like this, Wendy came up to where others were parking, so she parked off to the side of the others. Some were in the middle, and some were on the outside track, but she stayed on the outside and stopped the car. She took a deep breath, blew it out, let her shoulders relax against the back of the seat, shut off the engine, and closed her eyes.

"Congratulations!" Before Wendy could get out of the car, Sally was at her window and shouting, "Congratulations!" and a chorus of other voices echoed her.

Nearly pulling her out of the car, they kept yelling, "Good job!" and other praises.

Steve gave her a big hug and helped her pull her helmet off. Wendy asked," Why are you congratulating me? I'm not the one who won, Sally is." Wendy ran her fingers through her hair to get it out of her eyes.

"Sally always wins around here," one of the other drivers said, "so we don't count her." Other drivers laughed at that comment.

Something pulled on her left sleeve, and Wendy looked to see if it was caught on something, but it wasn't. The guy with the gray coat squeezed in and gave her a big hug.

"Congratulations! That's the closest this car has come to winning, and this lets me know what it can do. Thanks!"

Someone put a red ribbon in her left hand and shook her right hand while congratulating her. Voices were shouting and echoing in her head. "It's not fair!" someone shouted.

"Oh, get out'a here!" another responded.

A jerk on her right sleeve drew Wendy's attention, but all she could see was a button gone. Both sleeves hung loose with their buttons gone. The crowd was patting her on her back and was pushing and shoving her around, so she asked, "Where do we go from here?" She wanted to get away from their mauling hands.

"We have to wait until the judges finish passing out the ribbons, and then we can go up to the booth to collect the rewards," Sally said and continued, "Isn't this exciting?! I can't believe you came this close to beating me! No one has done that before, but you actually looked bored out there. I couldn't even see your hands on the wheel. Where'd you have them? You've been in races before, haven't you?"

"No, my father taught me that to relax, put my hands to the bottom of the wheel, and I'll have faster reflexes. Ow!!!" Someone had pulled a clump of hair from the back of her head and was claiming her reward as she jumped up and down in the crowd.

"Isn't there some place to go to get away from this crowd?" Wendy asked Sally.

"Nah, you'll get used to this after a while. They don't mean any harm."

Steve stayed close to her side, but he could not see what all the extra hands were doing. Wendy felt boxed in again. There had to be a way out of this. "How much of a reward does second place get?" she asked.

"Fifty dollars," Sally called back.

"Don't they get to you?" Wendy asked as someone pulled on the back of her shirt.

"They quit doing that to me a long time ago because I always win." Sally grinned.

"Who came in third?" Wendy asked as she rubbed the back of her head where her hair had been pulled out, and she looked at the blood on her hand.

"I did," one of the drivers off to the side said.

"What would happen if I gave my spot to her? Is that permitted?" Wendy asked. "Yes! Yes!" the third-place driver exclaimed.

"I don't know," Sally said, "I would have to ask Tony." With that, Sally disappeared.

Steve looked at Wendy, "You really wouldn't give up the spot, would you?"

"I need to get out of here," Wendy replied as more people started coming in from the bleachers.

"You should have seen the stands when you were going around the back turn. Some of them even came down off the bleachers and were getting closer to see everything and to be around when the drivers stopped," Steve continued. "They were going crazy! People were... Damn!" someone pulled his hair. "I see what you mean."

Sally pushed her way back up to them and said, "Tony says it's okay to pass your ribbon on."

The third-place driver squealed as the red ribbon was handed over to her.

Steve grabbed Wendy's arm as she started pushing her way out of the crowd. "Where ya goin'?"

"Stay here for me, please, and see if there is anything else I have to do. I have to get out of this crowd. I'll meet you on the bleachers." Wendy ducked as someone tried to grab her arm; then she cut through the crowd of people around her.

"There she goes!" Wendy could hear their voices as she squeezed her way through them. "That's her! Where's she goin'?"

Dodging elbows, Wendy ducked below many tall people until she wormed her way back to the bleachers. As she started climbing, she could hear two voices behind her.

"What are we following her for? She gave up her ribbon."

"I know, I have to tell her something."

"We should be down there..."

Stretching her legs from seat to seat to get away, Wendy finally gave up and sat down where she and Steve had been sitting before; the women kept coming. The one woman in the "AutoShop" jacket came slowly up to her while the one in the blue jean jacket with sequins on it stood back.

"Look, man, I'm sorry," AutoShop said as she stretched her hand forward. "I didn't mean to grab so much hair. I didn't mean to make you want to give up the ribbon. I mean..."

"That's okay. I know you didn't mean to do that. Don't worry; it wasn't the only reason I gave up the ribbon."

"Sorry," the AutoShop guy said again.

"Hey, come on! Let's get back down there," Blue Jean Jacket said.

Wendy was glad to see them turn and go back down. Their conversation mingled with the rest of the conversations in the bleachers.

"I feel ashamed of what we've been doing. She seems so nice," AutoShop said. "What do you mean?" Blue Jean Jacket asked.

"I wasn't very nice..." The last of AutoShop's words were inaudible, but others' rumbled up.

"That's her over there; I tell you!"

"What would she be doing here? She would be down there..."

"Quiet, she can hear us."

"I want to go over there."

Folding her hands in her lap, Wendy waited for Steve to finish with everything down there. It seemed to take him forever, and again the remote was on pause. One body blended in with another and became a moving mass of colors. She looked out towards the gate, wondered if she could find her way safely to the car, and stared in that direction. Moving very slowly, people were massed around the gate and made her feel more unsafe.

Steve tapped her on the shoulder, and she jumped. "Hey, you, okay?" He sat down beside Wendy and put his arm around her shoulder.

Unable to say anything, Wendy nodded. Too many feelings were flying around inside of her. She knew she didn't like fame and attention like that. That was not a success.

"Boy, did you have them all upset about the race you were in! They were going to cancel the awards for the race, but the other drivers gave them too much of a hassle, so they had to give them the money. The other race is already going, but no one is interested in it. Most of the drivers are the usual ones, and they pretty much know who is going to win. You ready to go?"

Wendy nodded; she had been ready for a long time. They worked their way down from the bleachers to the gate. There were fewer people here than up front, but she could still hear their surprised reaction when they recognized her. The car never looked so good as she slid into the front seat. Steve maneuvered the car nicely out of the parking lot and onto the road. Surprised by the fresh air coming from the vent, she curled her feet up under her. The air was no longer milky with dirt.

"I still can't believe that just happened!" Steve shook his head.

"Neither can I," Wendy mumbled.

"Did you want to do anything else tonight?" he asked.

"Nuh uh, I think I've done enough already. Let's just call it a night."

The next few days went by in a flash. They saw dolphin shows, wax museums, and street dances. Everything was beautiful, the weather warmed up, the gardens began to blossom, and this was more like the vacation Wendy wanted, but her mind kept going back to the race and her job she had quit. By the time her vacation was over and she had to leave, she was ready for the long road home.

Steve did not want her to leave and held onto her before he let her get into the car. Wendy watched Steve wave as she pulled the car onto the highway. She hoped he would not change when he came back from overseas. Saying a small prayer for both of their journeys, she watched the miles clip by.

With her hands calmly caressing the steering wheel rather than gripping it tight, Wendy realized she was back on the turnpike. The seat of the car did not fight her but cupped and relaxed her. The traffic was moderate, but few trucks passed her. There was one in front of her, and she realized the "How's My Driving" no longer laughed at her. As reality struck her, she wished she had rerouted herself back to avoid the turnpike, but the traffic was not bad, and the trucker left their boxes open.

The new job opening that one of the other LPNs told her about was a road out of a box. Wendy looked forward to going home.

# The Day is a Circle

Heat waves distorted the concrete landscape as Keane and Leigh walked up Santa Monica Boulevard. Unlike in the eighties temperatures last week, street signs no longer stood erect but reflected a misshapen reality that changed with every step they took. Leigh, always one or two steps behind Keane's long stride, took two steps to every one of his. She had learned quickly after they were married a year ago that complaining did not slow his pace, and right now, he was uncommunicative and upset because he had not heard from his friend Will. Messages had been left with everyone Keane could think of, but no one admitted to seeing or knowing Will. Lives go in circles, and what magic Will had for Keane was never revealed except as someone Keane would go drinking with, but Keane expected to get something big from Will.

Leigh's pregnancy stopped her from drinking with Keane at the bars, but not from his volatility, so she had not told him that she was pregnant again, just in case she wasn't and he got mad at her. Lately, Will's temper was ignited more frequently with the heat, and today's heat doused any hope of relief once they would get to the apartment, but at least Leigh would be off her feet and in some shade.

With so many people on the sidewalk, everyone was jamming into each other and shouting over the traffic. As the sidewalk ascended, it was easier to view people coming toward them, and Leigh watched as the pedestrians coming at them started thinning out as the swarm came over the hill. She hoped that it would stay that way, but the gap was soon closed up. People behaved differently here than she was familiar with in Seattle. Since she came to Los Angeles, she even saw a man who was walking down the street and holding a mirror in his hand; yelling obscenities to the mirror, he pointed his index finger at the image he saw in it. The people around him did not seem to notice anything different and kept on walking. Leigh was afraid to do anything about him, and Keane said, "Mind your own business."

It was nothing to smell marijuana while walking in the evenings, and today there was a terrible stench in the air. The sewers must have digested something unusually large and were belching the remains through the grates.

Usually, the smog carried enough chemicals in the air to make eyes burn and tear. Leigh watched as the people on the sidewalk continued to leave a nearly empty spot on the sidewalk, like Moses' water parting, around one woman walking towards them. She moved slowly and staggered from one side of the sidewalk to the other. As she got closer, Leigh could see that at one time the woman must have been fairly wealthy because she had a cashmere sweater on over her blouse, but both had seen cleaner days. As the woman came closer, Leigh realized that the smell was coming from the woman; people would get by her, realize that she was the skunk, and cross to the other side of the street. Keane started to step off the sidewalk, but Leigh stopped. There was something about the distorted image that Leigh recognized.

"Keane, there's something wrong with that woman. She needs some help." Leigh couldn't take her eyes off the woman.

"She's got a problem all right. She stinks!"

Leigh could see that the woman had a bruise on the left side of her face, peeking out from hair that resembled clay waves, and a triangular stain on the front of her skirt that might be blood. Leigh recognized the bloody stain of hemorrhage from a miscarriage, but did not remember any time when she was as dazed as this woman appeared to be. If the woman's stain was blood, it was also mixed with the feces that ran down her legs and pooled above her shoes inside her nylons. There was likely more occurring with this woman than what Leigh had experienced before. Maybe she was on dope. Leigh's mother had always taught her to stay away from street drugs, so Leigh never thought that would be a problem for her. "Don't get any ideas like taking in a stray cat. I don't want anything to do with her."

Keane grabbed Leigh's arm and pulled it towards the curb. When Leigh kept her eyes on the woman, Keane squeezed his fingers tightly around her forearm and yanked her off the curb. Leigh stumbled and fell toward Keane, and her arm wrenched and twisted. Keane held her from falling any further, and they crossed to the other side like the rest of the swarm.

Stealing a glance backwards, Leigh listened as the sirens screamed in the distance. They might be a mixed blessing. From her last hospital visit, Leigh and Keane were not able to pay the bill and had to move to hide from the collectors. Besides that, counselors had come into her hospital room and tried to tell her that life could be different. She tried to get Keane to go see them, but it only created more trouble. Their questions became more and more personal, even when they were on the phone. Leigh wasn't sure if she hoped that it was for the woman who was now attempting to cross a side street; she had fallen at the curb and was stopping traffic in the intersection. None were getting out of their cars to see if she was even breathing. They just sat there and waited for the ambulance to come. Wondering if she would want to be saved, Leigh looked at Keane and shivered.

Keane pulled Leigh around the corner of the next building, and she could feel him pinching the skin of her forearm between his fingers. Holding back tears and emotions, Leigh hung her head in submission and let him pull her along. Because they were no longer heading towards their apartment, she knew they were in for a long night.

They found Will with several of his friends sitting around him on the steps of an apartment building on Seventh Avenue. Once Will saw who was looking for him, he told the others they could leave, and Will went with Keane and Leigh to The Garden Bar. Nursing a Pepsi and scratching at the scabbed rash the doctors had told Leigh was from her nerves, Leigh sat quietly at the table while Will and Keane exchanged happenings, news, and rounds of beer. By the third round, Keane was very animated, and his hands did much of the talking with him, but Will barely sipped his beer and watched Keane closely. It was obvious that Keane was looking for a score, and Will did not appear to be interested in Keane's reminiscences of their hits. Politely, Will nodded his head and soon came up with an excuse to leave, but he promised Keane that he would get back with him and started to leave. As he went past Leigh, Will patted her shoulder and said, "Take care," and walked to the door.

Keane did not miss the action, and his smile was replaced with a glare at the other two.

Before Will was out of sight, Keane said, "1 didn't know you knew Will."

"I never met him before. Why?"

"Then why did he say that to you?"

"I don't know; maybe it's just his way. Are you ready to go?"

"No," Keane motioned for the waitress. "More beer here." Not another word was spoken while Keane drank another three beers and was sated enough to leave. As he got up, his steps faltered, and he bumped into the adjoining table. Leigh reached out her hand to steady him, but Keane brushed her away.

The night was a bit cooler as they made their way back to the apartment, but the heat in the apartment suffocated their first few breaths as they walked in. Once they got inside, Leigh went to the kitchen to make the coffee Keane always wanted when he came home from drinking. Keane went into the living room, turned the TV on loud, and sat glaring at the screen. It always surprised Leigh that neighbors never complained about its noise or what frequently followed.

Nervousness seemed to make Leigh's hands misbehave, and as she poured the coffee into the cup, she spilled some on the counter. Knowing what would have happened if he had seen that, she closed her eyes, and her lips moved silently, and then she cleaned the spill before he peeked around the corner. She steadied her hands on the counter and took a couple of deep breaths. Keane always wanted the cup as full as she could get it, and when she was afraid of him, it was hard for her to carry it so full and not spill it. One time, he spilled it for her and blamed it on her. She shivered in remembrance. That was the first time the stain had ruined her clothes, and that was why she recognized the marks on the woman earlier.

"Where in the hell is my coffee?" Keane yelled from the other room, and Leigh jumped.

She was glad that her hand wasn't on the cup just then and picked it up. Slowly, she walked into the living room and started to set the cup on the end table next to Keane's chair, but it was as if he read her mind, and he intercepted her path with his hand, making it difficult for her to pass the hot cup. As hot as it was in the apartment, the cup was even hotter, and it was hard to hold onto the cup, but she managed to get it into his hands before spilling any. He glared at her and then set the coffee on the table.

"Take my shoes off." Again, Leigh jumped at his terse words. "What's the matter with you tonight? Did you know Will before you met me? Is that why you are so jumpy?"

"No. I've never met him before. Really, it must be this heat." Leigh finished pulling off his shoes and stepped over to the open window, and looked out. "There's not even a breeze to cool things off."

"What? Don't mumble like that. If you've got something to say, say it."

Leigh wondered if she told him that she was pregnant, if it would change his sour mood, but it didn't stop him when she was pregnant the first time, and now Keane was already jealous of Will. Raising her voice above the TV, Leigh said, "It's just this heat; there's not even a breeze."

"You don't have to yell at me! I'm right here in the room." He snapped back at her.

"And I don't think it's the heat. You're feeling guilty about something. What did you do now?"

"Really, Keane, I've done nothing; I'm tired and hot, so I'm going to take a shower and go to bed. Is there anything else you want?"

"You're lying to me!" Keane stood up out of his chair. "What kind of trouble are you into now? Did you forget to pay the phone bill again?"

"No, please, Keane, I've done nothing wrong." Leigh backed away from his side of the room and started working her way toward the hall and the bathroom.

"Don't you back away from me like that!" He shouted. "What's the matter with you? I don't know why you behave the way you do."

Watching him come towards her, Leigh took another step backward and prepared to run if she could; however, there was nowhere for her to escape to.

He kept coming toward her and shouted, "And why can't you be more like other women and get pregnant again? It would be nice to have my own kid around me. At least he would be like me, and then I wouldn't have to deal with you all the time." Keane's speech was slurred, and he spat his words out with all the force of needles.

Leigh knew then that it would be useless to say anything about her pregnancy now because he would never believe her.

"You can't even bring me a decent cup of coffee!" His face was just inches from hers, and his spit was flying into her eyes.

Leigh closed her eyes as her foot reached the wall and could go no further. She knew what was coming next and slid down in a desperate hope of scooting away when he might overbalance, but his hand gripped her arm and held her fast while his other hit her face. She tried to curl up to protect her stomach, but somehow his foot found its way in with other blows, and she felt his foot hit its favorite spot around her bladder. This always seemed to make him feel better.

He laughed and said, "Go ahead and pee your pants bitch." Standing to his full height, he glowered above her.

Like every other time, Leigh lay on the floor and silently cried while he went to his chair and continued watching TV. If she made another sound, it might attract more wrath, which had happened last time. Her clothes were already soiled but were still salvageable if she could make it into the bathroom soon enough. As quietly as she could, Leigh pulled her body along the wall to the hall. Grabbing the arm of the couch near the door, Leigh pulled herself upright and half baby-stepped and scissor-stepped into the bathroom so that blood would not come squirting out.

The spasms had already started, so Leigh pulled her pants off and sat down carefully on the toilet. Waves of nausea almost sent her to the floor, but she turned sideways and put her head on the back of the toilet. Its wet coolness gave some physical relief to the windowless oven and helped her make it through the worst of the spasms. She filled the stool and flushed it three times, and hoped that all of the remains had come out. Otherwise, she would end up with an infection.

Because the door to the bathroom would not lock, she did not want to stay there too long and have him come in while she was like this. For once glad of the mini-room, Leigh reached over and turned the water on in the tub for a bath, and then grabbed the wash cloth from the sink. Pulling herself up, she wiped off as much as she could from the seat and put the cloth in the hamper. Picking up the Dixie cup from the counter, Leigh filled it with water and reached inside the medicine cabinet for the new medicine the doctor had given her. It was supposed to help calm her down and not feel so nervous, so it should also help with the pain she was feeling. She never used to take medicines, but it wouldn't hurt to do it now and then. Besides that, she was no longer pregnant, so it wouldn't hurt the baby. Finely, she stepped into the tub and eased herself into the water.

Her friend's words came back to her, and she knew what she should do; but with only an eighth-grade education, no one wanted to hire her, and she didn't want to go back to her family. That was one of the reasons why she got married a year ago when she was sixteen. Her father had been sleeping with her sister, so Leigh would hide in her closet at night and hoped that he would not find her and make her sleep with him. Leigh wondered what her mother thought of all of this. Leigh knew her mother was up in heaven but barely remembered her, and she wondered what her mother's life was like before she died eight years ago.

The noise from the TV was no longer voices but static, and Leigh heard Keane change the station and lower the volume. Most of the time, Keane, was not mean, and like he always told her, she 'had done something to rile him up.'

Reasoning things out, Leigh felt that her life could be worse than what it was; Keane never beat Leigh so much that she felt afraid for her life, so her life here wasn't all that bad. She had a roof over her head, Keane always brought home a paycheck, and they always had enough food. Leigh just needed to learn how to avoid his temper; her friend didn't agree with this, but what else could Leigh do? Light-headed from the medicine, Leigh started getting out of the cool water.

"Other women have it worse than me," Leigh had told her friend, but looking at her reflection in the mirror, Leigh wondered how others looked at themselves afterwards. Her right eye was black and blue, and something must have cut her cheek just below that eye. Probably his ring.

"With this ring, I thee wed... " Leigh wondered if she would do it again. Probably, but not to Keane. She couldn't remember anyone else, though, who had been interested in her. She always had to wear her sister's hand-me-downs; her dad could never alter them, so clothes draped over her until she grew into them, and they usually wore out before they fit right.

Resignedly, Leigh put her ripped nightgown on and opened the bathroom door. Keane was still in his chair but sleeping. Even though his snore belched alcohol into the air, he looked handsome like a hyperactive baby, looking peaceful to his mother when he was sleeping. Turning back down the hall, Leigh went to the bedroom and climbed into the big brass bed. He would be looking for her there in a little while. A perceptible breeze wiggled the sheer curtain, promising cooler temperatures and less tension. Like she read one time, "The day is a circle—morning, afternoon, and night." With her aches hidden from her right now, Leigh slipped into a desultory, dreamy sleep.

In the morning, Leigh found Keane still sleeping in his chair, so she went to the kitchen to start the usual oatmeal breakfast. With the radio close to the coffeepot, Leigh turned it on to lift the mood in the apartment. She liked listening to the local rock station because it made her feel like dancing. Leigh could hear Keane retrieve the paper from the mailbox and call, "Good morning," like she always did.

Keane came into the kitchen, sat at the kitchen table, and began rustling the paper while the radio announcer started the daily news. . . "A woman was found dead on the intersection of Santa Monica and Main streets yesterday, and her husband is..." Leigh was busy at the stove putting the cereal in dishes and pouring coffee. A usual beginning for a day.

# With It

"Sirena, be careful out there," Melva called through the open car window.

I turned around to look at the crew's manager to see if I had heard right. Rarely did she comment about the neighborhood we were selling in, and from all appearances, many of these apartments had expensive sports cars. It should be easy to make my quota within the next hour.

"What'cha worried about? Do you know something that I don't?" I asked as I leaned in through the passenger side window and fidgeted with the arms on the necklace as it bumped against the car.

"Not really, knock 'em dead." Melva flashed one of her go-get-em smiles. "Let's get done early today. See ya' in about an hour."

Stepping from the side of the road onto the sidewalk, I waved and watched the black Lincoln Mark V pull into traffic. In the past month, Melva had raised my quota twice so that I would not be able to meet her bonus. That rankled. Magazines were hard enough to sell door-to-door without quotas constantly going up. Sure, the crew had not been doing as good as Melva wanted it to, but I've been doing the best I can. Her Mark V may not be new this year, but Melva made things look worse than what they were.

Even though the apartments had security buzzers, it was easy to get people to open their doors. Bzzzzzt... Making sure that my purse was slung over my shoulder with my sales cards in it, I pushed a likely name, Jones, and waited a minute to let the person get to the intercom. I pulled my blond braid out from under my purse's shoulder strap and reminded myself to make myself look as young as 15 instead of my 20 years. When no one responded, I pushed another name, Cohen, which looked like it would not be too near the door of the one I had just pushed. Bzzzzzt.

"Hello." A man's voice responded.

"Hi, I just came over to see you for a minute," I said as my hand went up to my necklace.

The buzzer on the locked door rasped Grrrrrrrt, and I pulled the door open and double checked the number of the apartment for Cohen, 3B, and looked at the names of the other tenants to be able to drop their names if I needed to. Not bothering to look at the other apartments, I went up the stairs to the second door on the left. The door was already open, so I stepped across the door jamb to be sure to have my foot in the door to make it harder for someone to close the door. As I rapped on the door, I said "Hi," and took another step into the room. A tall man was standing next to a woman who was holding a handkerchief in her hand. "I'm Sirena, I came over to see you for a minute." Again, I paused to give them a chance to invite me in to sit so that I could start my spiel. When they just stood there without saying anything, I continued, "I'm with a group of young people in the neighborhood, and we are getting everyone around here to vote. You haven't voted yet, have you?"

"I didn't realize that there were any political elections going on right now. What's this all about?" the man said as he kept his arm about the shoulders of the woman standing next to him. His wrinkled suit hung crookedly, which made it look awkward. The room had a quietness to it that belied the sound of the TV coming from the door to my right. With the cutest jeans and plaid shirt on, a young boy of four or five was sitting Indian style in front of the screen, and it looked like he was rocking to some music.

Sitting like that, he reminded me of my third youngest brother, who had Down's syndrome.

This boy did not have the facial features that Down's typically has.

Two steps behind the couple was the living room, which had a white leather couch along the left wall, a white plastic end table, a love seat in the far corner, and a matching chair across from the couch. The entertainment center in the opposite corner housed one of the biggest television screens I had ever seen.

"Oh, this isn't voting for politics; it's for the local youth who are working on getting everyone's vote in order to win a contest and earn credits for a scholarship." I looked him carefully in the eyes to make eye contact and reached out my hand to act like I was going to touch him, but did not reach that far. "You haven't voted yet have you?" I declared.

"No, we haven't heard a thing about this. What's it all about?" The man asked.

"Here, why don't you come over here and sit?"

A movement from the woman caught my attention, and I caught her putting the hankie up to her face and dab at her eyes. As she did this, she sniffled and said, "John, I can't help it; I can't do this right now." Her soapy perfume was evident all about the room, but when she moved it was stronger.

"Honey, this is the best thing for you to do; you've got to start getting used to the idea and become more social again."

"Listen, if I've come at a bad time, please, I won't bother you. I'll just let myself out." I turned towards the door, but the man caught my arm.

"Wait, please." He turned to his wife and said, "Honey, this is just the kind of thing you need right now to get your mind off Hogan. You've been doing nothing but crying ever since we came home, and that's not good. You've got to snap out of this."

"I'm sorry if I've come at a bad time," I started again.

"We had some disheartening news about our son yesterday; they told us he's not normal, and Brenna has been crying ever since. She needs to divert herself. Go ahead and tell us what this contest is all about."

"What is going on with your son?"

"They tell us that he is autistic. It's some kind of mental disorder."

"I have a handicapped ' brother, so I understand how you feel. Sometimes, though. These problems that come up are..."

"Oh! He's not a problem!" Brenna dabbed at her red, blotchy face. "He's such a good boy, he never gives me any problems."

"What I meant is that it's hard to understand how others feel when they have to deal with someone having a disability. What is this disease he has?"

"He just sits there and rocks back and forth all the time. He never talks, but we can tell he's smart because he can do so many things. He can dress himself, and he never makes a mess. Ever. He's a good boy." Brenna sounded like she was trying to convince herself more than anyone.

"May I go in and talk to him?" I asked.

"He doesn't talk. We know he can because he understands everything we say to him, but he has never said a word to us," John said.

"Do you mind if I try? I've worked with my brother a lot, so I might be able to reach him." I looked at Hogan sitting in the other room and wondered what kind of illness he had. There was an article on the news not too long ago, but I couldn't remember too much about it. They said that it was like this person had chosen to go into their own little world and stay there. Even though they would cooperate with anything that you wanted them to do, they never interacted. Some of the ones they showed on television would bang their heads on a wall or something, and they had to wear a helmet to protect themselves from hurting themselves.

"Go ahead if you want to, but don't expect too much of a reaction from him."

He sat there about two feet from the TV screen and rocked back and forth on his butt. His right hand rolled something between his fingers, and his left hand seemed to stabilize his body on the floor, yet his fingers played with the fibers of the olive-green carpet underneath him.

Walking up beside him, I said, "Hi Hogan. How are you today?" I dropped down on the carpet beside him, and he barely altered his rocking pace. "What are you watching, Hogan?" Trying to think of questions, I pulled my pigtail behind my ear and looked closely at his face as it rocked. His eyes remained focused on the screen in front of him, and I wondered what he would do if I changed the station on him.

John and Brenna stood just to the side of the doorway watching what I was doing, and I asked,

"What does he do if you turn the station?"

"Nothing usually," John replied, "but sometimes he will reach up and put it back on the show he wants, but usually he waits until we leave, and then he puts his show back on. He knows what shows come on and when they come on. It's like he has some kind of internal clock or something."

I touched his arm. "Hogan, look at me." Moving my face between his face and the TV, I thought if I could make some kind of eye contact like we do in sales, I might be able to get some kind of reaction out of him.

"Hogan," I chanted his name. "HO-gan, HO-gan." Rubbing my hand on his arm, I continued to try to get his attention, but he always looked directly at the screen. I caught myself moving along with him as he rocked, and thought, maybe, if I got more on his level, to be just like him... Rocking. Keeping pace with his every movement. My left hand stabilizing and my right slightly bent at the elbow, "HO-gan," I called gently. "HO-gan."

His hand slipped into my hand, and we both sat there rocking, keeping pace with each other. There was a sound from behind us, but I could not make out what it was. Like Hogan, I felt safe where I was.

Emotionally feeling more than physically feeling, I thought no one would bother me here. Fear. It was here with ME. Inside, I must stay inside. I sensed him beside me, and we were rocking together. With fear. Primal. Do not go anywhere else. Stay.

NO! Don't let him pull! I must pull him!

Repeating in my mind, friend, gentle, friend, I slowed our pace, and he followed my lead. Slower. Slower. Stop.

"Hogan, I am you friend, Sirena." I called to him. Pointing to his chest, I said,

"Hogan." Then I pointed to myself and said, "Sirena. Friend."

He watched my hands, and then he looked at my face.

Again, I said, "Hogan," and pointed at him; then "Sirena," and pointed at myself. "Friends." Pushing fear to the side again, I picked up his hand and shook it; pointed my finger at him and said, "Friends." Then pointed at myself and said, "Friend."

"Friend."

It was just a small voice, but he said, "Friend!" "Hogan and Sirena are friends," I repeated. "Friends," he whispered.

I didn't know what else to say, and fear was pulling me until I was seeing dark spots in front of my eyes. I was afraid to continue, but I was just as afraid to stop. I closed my eyes and thought of as many pleasant thoughts as I could. When I opened my eyes again, I could see better. Hogan's eyes were wide. He looked straight at me, and the whites of his eyes shone around his black irises. A strand of black hair had fallen over his left eye, and his hand came up to brush it away.

Shaking my head, I felt someone's hand touching my arm. Looking down, I thought it would be Hogan's, but it was his father's.

"Are you okay?" he asked.

Nodding my head, I looked at Hogan, but he was back rocking, so I tried to move. Energy was gone. Arms felt like they had fifty-pound weights in them. Legs tingled with pins and needles as I moved them from under me. My head hurt, and IT was still there. Inside of me, I felt that fear. Looking at Hogan, I could see him looking back at me. He had stopped rocking, but he knew I knew. Forcing my legs to move, I stood up and looked at his parents.

Brenna was standing there with her back to the wall. Tears were flowing freely from her burning, red eyes. Her hands were steepled in front of her mouth as she kept repeating, "He spoke… He Spoke…"

John's grin broke through my haze, and he looked like he was the happiest man in the world. Standing taller, he seemed to fit the Hudson suit he wore so perfectly; he was like a picture in the catalog, his arm draped around his wife's shoulders, as if cloaking her from the chilly air that I felt.

Stumbling to the door, I mumbled, I did the best I could; it wasn't much, but I tried to communicate with him, and all I could get out of him was one word."

"But that is much more than anyone else has ever done!" Brenna exclaimed!

"This is the first time he has ever spoken to anyone! He has said his first words." They were both celebrating, but I found it hard to celebrate with them. IT was still here with me. I needed to leave before I could not. "I have to get going now."

"No problem!" They chorused. "And of course we will vote for you. How do we do it?"

Pulling out the sales cards, I shoved them in their paws and said, "You need to buy some magazines."

"Of course!" they smiled at me.

Without saying a word, I gave them the forms to fill out.

"Are you okay?" John asked

"Just drained, is all," I mumbled. "I need to get going because my manager will be looking for me." I turned toward the door, which still stood open, and before I could take a step, John put a check in my hand and shook the other.

"Thank you so much! You've done so much for us. You'll never know…"

"I think I do," I replied. There was a tug on my arm, and I turned back towards

Hogan's room, and he was at my elbow. Looking at me. I bent down and gave him a hug. "Goodbye, friend."

"Friend."

I walked out with IT.

# Peanut Butter Kid

As my house came into view, I snuck up to the front of the school bus. I hoped Mrs. Becker wouldn't notice that I was out of my seat before the bus stopped. I sprinted down the steps and up the driveway before she could make me stop. The old house needed a fresh coat of paint. And I knew I would be elected to do it when summer came, but for now, I needed to earn money for the prom. As I pulled the door open, the smell of a roast in the oven made my mouth water. It's too bad I had to work tonight and miss Mom's famous meal.

"Hi, Mom!" I called as I ran up the stairs, threw my books down in the bedroom, and went to the bathroom.

"How was school today?" Mom's muffled voice came up through the register in the floor. When we were kids, we used to talk to each other from the first floor through the registers to the second floor like phones.

"Fine," I called back. "I have to work tonight, so I won't be here for supper."

"Where do you work..." Mom's muffled voice was drowned in running water.

I'll go down later and tell her, I thought. Paul wants to go to the movies tonight, but I need the money to get my dress. Oh, it is so beautiful! My friend Terri and I found it when we went to the mall three days ago. Everyone knew that Paul and I would go to the prom together. We'd dated for the past two years, even though he was a year older than me. Even before he asked me, I put a down payment on the dress, and now I had to pay it off.

The telephone rang, and Mom answered it downstairs and then called for me to answer it. Mom and Dad finally gave in and let me have my own phone last year; it was the old one from downstairs, but it was better than nothing. Paul was on the other end, making small talk like he had something else on his mind.

"What's the matter, Paul?" I looked at my watch, which Mom gave me for my birthday. The small hands showed 3:45. Mrs Harris would be coming in fifteen minutes.

"Nothing. Are you sure you can go to the movies with me tomorrow morning?" His voice sounded different to me.

"Yeah, why?" I knew he was upset earlier because I told him that I had to work tonight.

"I don't know, I guess it's just that you've been so busy lately that we never seem to get to do anything."

"I want to earn a little extra money to get that dress for prom." We had this conversation before, so it puzzled me to hear him like this. "Listen, I have to get ready to babysit tonight, so why don't you call me there later?" I picked up the brush and began running it through my long, dishwater blonde hair.

"You sure it's okay?" he asked. "I mean, you won't get into trouble for being on the phone."

"Not if we talk only for a little while."

"Okay, I'll call you later, then."

"Okay, bye," I said, and hung up the receiver.

Finishing up with my hair, I tossed the brush on the counter and glanced at the mirror. It would do for tonight, but I'd have to get it done for the prom. Unzipping the book bag, I pulled out the paper that needed editing. I could do it

94

while I was at work and the baby was sleeping. I grabbed my coat and purse; nothing else to do up here. I sprinted down the stairs, dropped the paper and my purse in the living room chair, and went into the kitchen. Mom was working at the sink, fixing a salad. She still had the same youthful look she had when her prom picture was taken.

"Mom, do you think I'll look as pretty as you do when I'm your age?"

"Of course, Stacy, but I don't look as pretty as I did then. What was that compliment for anyway?" She turned to me, her hands still wet from the lettuce, and began chuckling as I grinned.

"Nothing. I just hope I will look as good as you do."

Mom's appearance was a constant joke between us. She was very pretty, and I felt I took after her. The girls at school envied our dark brown almond-shaped eyes. I was glad that I didn't end up with Dad's features; his nose alone would make Jimmy Durante jealous.

"I want to show you the dress that I put on layaway at Marian's, but I have to babysit at Mrs. Harris tonight, and tomorrow I'm going with Paul to the movies—How about going with me Sunday?"

"That would be okay after church, as long as your father doesn't have something else going on." She turned back to the salad and finished putting the lettuce in the bowl.

"What can I fix real quick before I go?" I opened the refrigerator door to see if there were any leftovers.

"The last of the chili disappeared at lunch when Dad came home between meetings, so you'll have to make a sandwich or something."

Grabbing the peanut butter from the cupboard and the bread from the breadbox, I began fixing the sandwich. Brad, my dear brother, used to call me the Peanut Butter Kid.

"Mom, what are you and Dad doing tonight?"

"Dad has to go to a meeting at the fire department, and I am going to Aunt Betty's." Finished with the salad, she put the lettuce container in the refrigerator.

Dad was one of the volunteer firemen in the community and had to go to the meetings at least once a month. He was also a medical technician for the department and taught first aid to the public. I was proud of my parents. Not too many kids at school felt this way. They were always good to us kids, but also let us make our own mistakes. A year ago, I would have given two cents to anyone who would take them, but now things looked different.

With a sandwich in hand, I went into the living room, turned on the TV, and waited for Mrs. Harris to come. She was a teacher at the high school, and I was one of the fortunate few she asked to babysit for her. She had a three-month-old who was like taking care of a doll because she was so good. Only half finished with my sandwich, I heard the familiar toot outside and hurried to get my stuff together and run outside.

Mrs. Harris's candy apple red Caprice was pulled in front of the house, and its motor was running. Holding the sandwich in my mouth, the paper in my hand, and my purse slung over my shoulder, I opened the door with my other hand, climbed in, and pulled the door shut.

"You didn't have to eat and run like that; you could have eaten at our house." She pulled carefully from the curb and onto the street.

"That's okay," I said with a mouthful of peanut butter, sticking my words together.

She laughed, "Thanks for coming to babysit on such short notice."

I was just glad to have the opportunity to earn more

They paid the best of any of my babysitting jobs that I had.

As she drove, Mrs. Harris said, "The baby has been a little fussy today, but you shouldn't have too much of a problem. I gave her a dose of liquid Tylenol; it could be her teeth coming through. There isn't more of the Tylenol, but I should be home before she needs more. I'll pick up more on the way home..."

She had a way of talking a lot, so half the time I tuned her out but listened if there was anything important. Liked by all the kids in school, her intelligence showed in her attentive students. Driving into the cul-de-sac of their subdivision, she continued chatting while I looked at their manicured lawn. I loved working there and sitting in their living room and looking out at all the flowers they had in their backyard. She stopped the car next to a flowering Rose of Sharon, and we went into the house. She showed me where the phone numbers were in case I needed to call her, and what the baby might need for the night. She was still talking as she and her husband walked out the door.

Sleeping, the baby was in her crib and looked like a little doll with her ruffled onesie on. Since it was only a little after four, I sat at the kitchen table working on my paper. The good shows came on around seven, and by that time, I could have most of it done. I didn't expect the Harrises back until after midnight, since they had to go out of town for a business dinner. Things were pretty quiet, so I was able to get a lot done on my paper until the baby woke up at 6:30. Usually, she woke up and just kind of whimpered, but this time she cried, so I changed her diaper and fixed a jar of baby food. She was fussy and wouldn't eat, so I went into the living room, held her on my lap, and turned the TV on. Their living room was one that could have been seen in a magazine. The floor was sunk two steps to the main part, with a field stone fireplace on the outside wall by the garage. The other outside wall had three large bay windows looking into the back yard, which still showed remnants of summer's garden.

The baby was still fussy, so I held her on my lap facing me, made funny faces at her, and chanted, "Carrie... Carrrriiee, what's the matter with Carrrriiee?" but that didn't seem to make too much of a difference. Her face was flushed, and she looked very uncomfortable. Carrying her in my left arm, I went to the kitchen and prepared a bottle of sugar water, hoping it would give her something to chew on and soothe her mouth. She didn't even seem to want it. Patting her back, I sat in the living room with her on my shoulder. The TV game show host was reciting a question to the contestants, but I couldn't hear it over Carrie's cries.

The phone rang, and I hoped it was the Harrises, but Paul's voice came on the line with the same hesitancy it had before.

"Paul, oh, hi. I can hardly hear you, the baby is crying. Something is wrong with her. She's really fussy. I wish Mrs. Harris would call so that I could find out what to do to settle her down."

"And here I thought you would be glad to hear from me." His voice sounded hurt.

"I am, but the baby's so fussy; she won't stop crying. This has been going on for the past hour." I held Carrie in one arm, the phone between my shoulder and ear, and the bottle in my other hand while trying to get her to put it in her mouth so I could hear what he was saying.

"With the kid?" he asked.

"What did you..." I started, but the phone dropped from my shoulder, so I put the bottle down and picked up the receiver. I got it up to my ear as I heard the phone go "CLICK."

"Darn." I looked at Carrie, who was still crying as if she had a pin stuck in her.

After rechecking her diaper, I tried to give her the bottle again, but nothing seemed to work. She felt warm, so I checked to see if there was anything in the medicine cabinet. Nothing there. Talk about "Old Mother Hubbard" going to her cupboard. The other bathroom had all the things adults would use, from aftershave to cold medicine, but nothing for a child.

Carrie was screaming so loud that I thought if she didn't hurt from anything else, her throat probably hurt from crying. I felt like shaking her to make her stop, and I held her at arm's length, wanting to shake her. But I couldn't. I knew it wouldn't do any good. Pulling her close to my shoulder, I patted her back and started walking with her leaning against my shoulder. She kept lifting her head up and pulling at anything her little hands could reach, including my hair. I should have tied it back somehow when I was at home. I walked from the bathroom to the kitchen.

Everything was decorated in pastel colors, with eggshell-white walls and pink wine-colored trim. Even the carpeting was eggshell white with pink flowers and green leaves. The curtains matched the carpeting and fell from their rods in even pressed pleats. The phone sat on the counter and was the same color of pink. After picking up the phone list Mrs. Harris left for me, I picked up the phone, held Carrie in the crook of my arm, and dialed the first number on the list.

"Grandt's Restaurant," the anonymous voice said.

Talking above Carrie's cries, I said, "I'm trying to find Mr. or Mrs. Joseph Harris. They were at the employee dinner party for Davis Tool and Dye Company. Would you check to see if they are still there?"

"I'm sorry; they left already; not even giving me time to say, thank you," he hung up.

I looked at the grandfather clock in the corner. Its mahogany wood reflected the light from the dining room. They had left here at four-thirty, and now it was eight. The second number on the list looked like someone's name. Juggling the baby and the phone, I got the number and dialed. It rang five times, but there was no answer. With no other number on the sheet, I put the phone down.

Now, Carrie was crying and hiccuping at the same time. *The poor kid,* I thought, *Maybe I can find Mom.*

I dialed our number, and when there was no answer, I dialed Aunt Betty's number. Still no answer. I've got to think of someone who can help, I thought. Someone has to be around somewhere! But I have to go to the bathroom before I do anything else. What next?

I put Carrie in her crib, and she screamed louder. I was in the middle of going when the phone rang. Oh God! Please let it be Mrs. Harris. I quickly stopped, ran to the phone, and

100

picked it up in time to hear a tape recording about having my house windows done. Spamming the phone, I went back to Carrie.

She was just whimpering now, but her face was very red, and she still hiccuped. As I lifted her up, I noticed something greenish-red on the sheet in her crib. I looked at Carrie's face, but I couldn't see anything right away. Turning her face to the side, I noticed there was a trace of red crusting where something had drained out of her right ear. All kinds of things went through my mind. From the movie about space aliens that took over human brains through their ears to the idea that Carrie could lose her hearing from an ear infection, ideas raced as I picked Carrie up.

We went back into the kitchen, and I straightened the crocheted white blanket that was around Carrie. Underneath the blanket, Carrie's pink foot of her sleeper kept peeking out of the bottom of it. I stood by the phone and tried to think of whom I could call for help.

Maybe I could find the number of the fire station and call Dad!

Juggling Carrie again, I looked for the phone book. Most people kept them under the phone, but there wasn't one there or in the drawer under the phone. Finally, I found it inside the nightstand in the bedroom, where there was another phone. Lying Carrie on the bed, I flipped through the pages to the emergency numbers and found the number of the fire station.

Carrie kept whimpering, but at least she wasn't screaming like she had been. The voice on the receiver sounded vaguely familiar, but I couldn't remember who it was.

"Is Mr. Durand there?"

"No," the voice curtly replied.

"This is his daughter, and I need to talk to him. This is an emergency."

"He's at the meeting over in the township hall. Do you have the number?"

"No. Just a minute; let me get a pencil." I rummaged in the drawer of the nightstand and couldn't believe that there was one there. "Okay, go ahead."

"543-9328."

"Thank you." After pushing the button down, I quickly dialed the number. I looked at Carrie on the bed. She wasn't even whimpering. Just lying there, her eyes half open, and her face a reddish pink, almost as red as the time Brad got so sunburnt he ended up in the hospital. The receiver kept ringing. I started to count the rings. One... Two... Three... I noticed a sickly sweet smell around Carrie. I wondered if that meant she had some kind of problem with diabetes. Grandma used to smell when her blood sugar went high or low. This didn't smell like that, though. Fourteen... Fifteen... This is ridiculous! I might as well forget it. I started to hang up when the line clicked, and a voice came on.

"Hello."

"Could I please speak to Mr. Durand? He's in the meeting with the firemen."

"Just a minute." The deep voice barely stopped when I heard the familiar click of the phone being placed on hold.

The heat radiated from Carrie, and I knew she needed something, but I wasn't sure what I should do. I just sat there. She just lay there, breathing very fast and not moving. I didn't know what scared me more, her not moving or her screaming the way she had earlier. Finally, I heard Dad on the phone. I couldn't hold it anymore. I started crying.

"Hello, who is this?" he said.

"Daddy, I'm at the Harrises," I sobbed. "The baby is sick, and I don't know what to do."

"Calm down. What seems to be wrong with her?"

She cried from six-thirty until about fifteen minutes ago; then, all of a sudden, she stopped. I noticed some stuff draining from her ear. Now all she does is just lie there, not moving.

"I can't find the Harrises." The words seemed to tumble out as if I couldn't control them.

"Okay." His voice seemed to take on a lecture tone. "Have you given her any kind of medicine?"

I started to feel better. At least someone else could help me. "She had some before they left some Tylenol, I think, but there isn't any more here. Mrs. Harris said she had to pick some up on her way home tonight."

"You try to get the Harrises again. Then give the baby a sponge bath with water that feels just about the same temperature as your elbow or a little cooler. I'll be there in a few minutes." Then the phone went dead in my ear.

I picked up Carrie, went to the kitchen where the numbers were, and dialed the second number again. No answer. I carried Carrie to the bathroom and began running the water. As I got her sleeper off, I noticed that her whole body was red, and wherever there was a fold of skin, it turned white. At first Carrie just lay there and let me put the washcloth on her and she didn't move. Then she started to shiver and move around in just a few minutes.

The phone started ringing, so I grabbed Carrie and the towel at the same time and ran to the phone. "Hello," I was praying that it was the Harrises.

"Hi, Stacy," Paul said. "It sounds like the baby is doing better."

"Oh, Paul, you wouldn't believe it! She cried for almost two hours straight, then this stuff started draining from her ear. I called Dad, and he's on his way."

"It sounds serious," his voice was flat, like the way he sounded when he talked to his parents.

"It has to be. Dad sounded upset when I described her to him on the phone. He had me give her a cool bath, and she started looking a little better. I..."

"Listen, Stacy," Paul interrupted. "I called to tell you that I'm not going tomorrow, and I'm not going with you to the prom."

"What?" I couldn't believe it! We'd always gone together! "Why not?"

"Things aren't the same as they were. You've changed, maybe I've changed, I'm not sure. But it's over for us. Goodbye." Then the phone started buzzing.

Tears came out. Silent tears. I sat on the chair and rocked Carrie in my arms. She lay there like a rag doll. Not moving. The tears fell onto her face. Her face would come clear, then blur again as the tears welled in my eyes.

"No," I whispered as I rocked. "No, oh no!" Everything for nothing. My life's gone. What had I done? I rocked. Nothing else could be done.

BANG, BANG, BANG.... BANG, BANG, BANG. Startled, I jumped and almost dropped Carrie. I had forgotten about her. Clutching her close, I ran to the door and opened it.

"Let me see her." Dad grabbed Carrie from me. "Try to get the Harrises' again." He ran to the bathroom and started running the water. The door remained open as I went to the phone, and it seemed like I was in slow motion. My mind wouldn't work. Where were the numbers? They were here a minute ago.

Picking up the sheet from the floor, I began dialing the number on the bottom. One ring... two... "Hello."

"Oh, please, is Mr. or Mrs. Harris there? This is their babysitter."

"No, but they should be here in a few minutes. They were right behind us..."

"Their baby is really sick. I called my father, and he's here now, but we need to talk to them."

"Just a minute; I think they're here now."

I could hear the phone being put down. "Daddy! I think I've got them on the phone," I called out.

A muffled sound came from the bathroom, then he came in carrying Carrie in a towel. He put her gently in my arms and took the phone.

"Hello," he said as he looked at me.

"Someone went to get them, they're outside." Carrie didn't feel as hot, but she still lay there like a doll. I looked at Carrie and could see she still had that lifeless look. God, no! Don't let anything happen to her! Dad's voice was in the background, and his face was angry-looking.

"Needs more than what I can do." Silence held my attention as he listened to someone on the other end. His black hair fell in his face, and he wiped it away with an impatient swipe.

"Okay." He pushed the button on the phone down with his finger and let it up right away. Then he began dialing a number memorized by frequent use. I watched as he stood there so calmly, but his eyes sparkled, and his lips were tight in a thin line. "Hello, this is Bill Durand. We need an ambulance at Joseph Harris' house. What's the address here?"

I looked at him blankly. "I don't know, just a minute; they keep their bills here in a drawer... It's 3425 Lincoln."

Listening to him repeat the number, I noticed that Carrie was moving, so I shifted the towel to see her face better. I screamed, "Daddy!"

Daddy dropped the phone and grabbed Carrie from me. Her limbs were shaking spastically. Her lips were closed in a tight line, and her face was starting to turn blue. Daddy put his face over hers and started blowing in her nose as he held her at an odd angle. He's going to break her back! I thought wildly, but I knew that what he was doing was right. Sirens started breaking through the scene before me. The screech of tires as the ambulance came around the corner of the driveway came through the open door.

I should do something, I thought, but what? I looked at Daddy and saw he was intent on what he was doing. I couldn't move. Car doors slammed, and muffled voices came from the front door. The ambulance personnel came in the front door and began doing their work. I saw everything, but I saw nothing. Tears slid down my face as I stood there looking. I couldn't move. All of a sudden, I felt Daddy's arm around my shoulders.

"They'll take care of her, now. Don't worry."

They worked together, but separately, each doing his own job. It seemed like it took a long time for them to help Carrie. They each knew what to do and did it without saying more than they had to. More car doors slammed. The Harrises came in as the attendants worked on Carrie.

"Oh my God! Carrie!" screamed Mrs. Harris. Things became a blur. I felt like it was all my fault. I backed into a corner of the room and stood there, watching all that went on. Mrs. Harris screamed until one attendant told her husband to shut her up. Then he took her into the other room.

"We've got to get her to the hospital or we're going to lose her." The tall attendant said to the red-haired one. The words burned in my ears. My face felt hot.

"Let's do it. It'll take two of us just to work on her on the way, so I'll call for help."

"I can drive, if you want some help," Daddy said. "I'm a fireman and drive their trucks, so I have plenty of experience." Red Shorty nodded to the tall attendant. Shorty went into the bedroom to tell the Harrises. I stood there in the corner.

"Stacy," Dad said. "Stacy.... You okay?" He gently wiped my face with his handkerchief.

I looked up at him but couldn't say anything. The attendants were working in the room, and the sounds of them frightened me. I stood there and tried to force myself to get control, but my knees gave out; then everything went black.

There were sounds that came to me, and then the blackness started going away.

Something stung my nose and smelled like alcohol, but worse.

"Stacy… Stacy." Daddy's voice sounded far away and slowly became louder. "You okay now?"

My eyes were open now, but the face in front of me wouldn't come into clear.

Blinking my eyes several times helped me get in focus. I started to look in the direction from which the other noises were coming, but Daddy kept my head looking toward him.

"Carrie is still sick, but she's alive and okay for now. Don't look over there because there are a lot of tubes and stuff. You're close to being in shock yourself, and your blood pressure is a bit high, so we're going to take you to the hospital to get checked over. You'll be riding in the ambulance, but not the one Carrie will be in. Just stay right there and keep looking this way."

His voice droned on, and I could feel the tightening of the blood pressure cuff on my arm. "Your mother is already on the way to the hospital, so she'll be there by the time we get there." His face showed concern and kindness to me, but when he looked up at what was happening in the rest of the room, it showed something else. Soon, I heard the sounds of the attendants taking Carrie out of the house and to the ambulance.

A different set of attendants came into view and helped me get onto the stretcher. As they wheeled me out to the ambulance, Daddy kept talking to me, and I started feeling a little better even though my head hurt. I had a hard time paying attention to what he said, but I was glad he was there, saying something. All kinds of scenes started flying before me: the night sky, the inside of the ambulance, and my father's face.

They pulled me out of the ambulance, and the wheels of the stretcher dropped down with a thud. The ride was rough as they wheeled me over the cement ramp to the emergency room. Quickly, the night was blinded by the harsh lights of the building, and time started to catch up with me, but Daddy's face was always there. Just when I needed him, he was there. He was always saying something reassuring to me and confident that everything would be okay.

Mom was already in the hall as we got to the cubicle where we were to wait. A nurse came in and left after getting my temperature and other things, but Mom or Dad never let my hand go. Brad had come in with Mom, and he stood over in the corner of the cubicle by the dividing curtain. "You did the best you could have done, so let's talk about it if you can," Dad said.

I nodded my head, but words had a hard time coming out. Tears started again, and Mom wiped them with a tissue. I couldn't stop the tears. They were silent. I was afraid to open my mouth for what would come out. I had no right to cry like Mrs. Harris did. It was her child, not mine.

Mom gave me a big hug and said, "Go ahead and cry as much as you need to. She held on as long as I let her stay there, but my nose started to drip, so I started reaching for a tissue.

After blowing my nose, I tried to ask how Carrie was, but could only croak, and that made more tears come. I don't remember how many times I repeated this, but then I finally managed. "Carrie?"

"We don't know yet," Mom said. "They're over in another part of the emergency room. Mr. Harris promised he would let us know. He's worried about you, too. As soon as you feel okay, we'll let them know. They're in a waiting room because the staff said they needed the room to work in."

"Thank you, I love all of you!" I wanted to say more, but couldn't. Mom and Dad stayed there. holding on, and Brad moved up by the foot of the cart with his hands touching inches from my feet. I felt like we were holding on to each other, and to Carrie.

A man, in a gray tweed suit covered by a white coat, came in. "Hi, I'm Dr. Paterson, and I need to ask you some questions about how Carrie's illness started."

I nodded my head.

She started crying at 6:30, and by 7:30 or 8, I was trying to get the Harris, but I couldn't. Paul called at 7:30, and it was just after that that Carrie had the drainage from her ear.

"Well, once we get the fever under control, she should be okay. I believe Dr. Mason has the seizures under control already. He's the one who will be taking care of her until her family doctor comes in." As he was saying this, Dr. Paterson was looking in my ears and eyes and checking my pulse. Your blood pressure has come down, and you look like you are feeling better." He turned to my parents and said, "I want her to stay here just a little longer to make sure her vital signs stay stable; then she should go home and take it easy; keep her in bed tomorrow."

"Okay," Mom said. "You hear that, Stacy, nothing going on for tomorrow."

I thought of what I was supposed to do tomorrow, and that brought more tears. No one else knew what had happened, and they thought the tears were for Carrie, and some were. Some were also for Paul.

"If this keeps up, we may have to keep her in here for a while more than just tonight." Dr. Paterson looked at me and put his hand under my chin and said, "'No matter what happens, you did all you could have. You probably did more than what many others would have. Quit worrying about it because I'm sure she'll be okay."

I nodded my head, and he pulled the curtain behind him as he left the cubicle. I looked at Mom. "I won't be going tomorrow... or to the prom," I said, and I gulped back more tears.

Mom came close to me and put her arm around me. "What happened?"

I shook my head and got enough control to continue. "Paul's been different ever since I started trying to earn money for the prom dress. Said we changed. Yes, I've changed, but I thought he loved me. He said we were through."

Mom held me close, Dad held my hand, and Brad's face turned red. What would I have done if they weren't around? The more I got closer to them, the more I began to appreciate them. To think I would have given them away a year ago.

"I love you guys so much! What would I have done tonight without you?"

"We love you, too!" Mom said, and Dad squeezed my hand. "You know you'll always have us there when you need us."

"Don't worry about Paul." Brad said, "I bet there are quite a few guys who will be glad to take you. Even I would be proud to take you."

"Oh, Brad," I laughed and cried at the same time. I wiped my face off and sat on the side of the cart. It was supposed to be a bed for the emergency room, but I would have hated to see a really big person on it.

"Listen, I'm going out to see how..." Dad started to say, but was cut short.

"No!" A screech could be heard that brought goose bumps and tears at the same time. Daddy started out through the curtain, but the nurse, shaking her head, turned him back around. No one needed to say anything else.

We knew what had happened. I looked up at the nurse. "Please, may I go see Mrs. Harris and say something to her?"

"Let me check." The nurse stepped out of the cubicle.

"Stacy, I don't think you should..." Dad started saying.

I held up my hand. "It's okay, Dad. I'll always have you, but they just lost her. I'd like them to know how I cared."

The nurse came in shaking her head. Mrs. Harris isn't up to having anyone there right now. The doctor is with her."

Dr. Paterson came in, "Get her vitals, please." Turning to me and picking up my hand, he said. "I'm sorry, but she didn't make it."

The tears came down my face, but not like they were before. It was like some part of death was locked up now. A part that could be taken care of in the future.

The nurse handed Dr. Paterson the chart and left the room. The doctor turned to Mom and Dad. "She may go home now. Her vitals are staying stable. I'm surprised." Then he turned to me. "Nothing tomorrow. Stay home and stay in bed. You can talk to Harris some other time when both of you can handle it better."

Mr. Harris came in. I was surprised. He had tears in his eyes, but not on his face. "He's told you, then." He held up his hand as the doctor started to open his mouth. "No, Stacy, you did a good job there with everything. There was nothing more that you could have done, but my wife is pretty upset."

"Mr. Harris, I feel so bad. Is there anything I can do to help? Even if it's just cleaning. I wish there was something I could've done before," I rambled on.

"Please," he interrupted. "I want you to understand; I think it would be easier on her if she didn't see you for a while, and she can cope with it better. Remember, neither one of us blames you."

I started to say, but he turned with tears running down his face, and left the room.

Mom and Dad stood there next to me, and Brad came around in front of us and said, "I'm going to have to stop calling you The Peanut Butter Kid if you are going to the prom. You're getting too old for that."

I knew what would happen at the prom. "I would be proud to go with you, Brad, but you would feel uncomfortable there, and you know how the other kids would talk. I'll ask some of the other kids at school." I thought, I still have the rest of my life to live, Carrie doesn't. I'll make mine live.

# Reactions to Down's Syndrome

When we react to various situations, we often fail to consider the consequences of our actions or the impact of our words. I was on a bus coming home when I started getting tired of riding. We were about an hour from Las Vegas, and I had been on a bus for almost eight hours. In eight hours, there are many things to think about, and at this point in my life, I have many things to think about. A divorce is a difficult concept to consider, and since I was seven months pregnant, it made the concept even more difficult. Returning home to my family in this condition was hard to do, but to make a step like that was even harder. Because I was tired of riding, I decided to get up and walk up to the driver and talk to him for a while. I had no problem keeping my balance on the bus because the highway was deserted at three o'clock in the morning. I made it to the front and said, "It's been a long ride so far, and I have a long way to go, you don't mind if I stand here and talk to you for a few minutes, do you?"

"I don't mind at all, as long as it's not hard for you to stand there and not fall and hurt yourself. How long have you been riding?"

"I started out in Los Angeles and headed to Saginaw, Michigan, so I know I've got a long way to go."

"That's for sure. Not much traffic right now, so it gets kinda' boring just sitting there." He kept his eyes on the road, and all I could see of him was the whites of his eyes in the mirror and the curly hair on the back of his head.

We talked small talk for just a few minutes, and at one point, he turned his head to look directly at me. "No! You're not." He started saying, but I interrupted him.

114

"Don't worry, I'm not having any pains or problems. I'm just fed up with riding." I felt bad because I had not let him know that he had a pregnant woman on board, and here I was standing there looking very much a butterball--as wide as I was tall--and very obviously pregnant.

"Are you sure? I've heard other guys talk about experiences like this that they've had, and I know nothing about delivering. If you're having problems, I can call for help, but I can't do anything." The words were coming out spitfire fast, and I had a hard time reassuring him. I can't even remember what all I said to reassure him, but I don't think I was very effective at it. It wasn't even five minutes later, and he was slowing the bus and stopping along the side of the road. "We're not permitted to smoke on the bus when we're driving, and I feel like I need to have a cigarette. You sure you're okay?"

"Yes, I'm fine. Look, I'll go back and sit down if that will make you feel better."

He hopped off the bus and headed for some bushes, and I went back to my seat. I felt bad because I had scared him so bad, and after that, I made sure the driver knew I was on board before we left the station.

We all have difficult situations like this that we have to react to. When my daughter, Sirena, was born with Down Syndrome, the first reaction that I had was fear. She was supposed to be in the room with me all the time, and the nurses would not let me have her there the morning after delivery. They kept giving me excuses like, "The doctor wants her kept under the Bili light. Many babies who are born need this because their bilirubin is high, and this helps reduce it."

"Does this mean there is something wrong with my baby?"

There it was, a mother's worst fear, facing me like a huge shadow of a mountain.

"No, the doctor will be in to talk to you in a bit. You will have her in here after he comes in to see you."

It seemed like the wait was forever. The nurses would not let me go to the nursery and kept saying that the doctor was on his way. But because he was up delivering my daughter at midnight, he didn't come until almost noon. When he walked in and pulled a chair close to the head of my bed, I felt the fear bigger than a wave. I couldn't say a word--he took a deep breath--one like when you start tackling a job you don't want to do--but I was already crying before he said his first word. "Someone has already told you then?" I shook my head. After a long silence, he said, "She has what we call Down's Syndrome. Do you know what that is?"

Again, I shook my head; I could not say anything because of crying. "It is also called Mongoloidism. Are you familiar with that?"

I knew this because some of my parents' friends have a child like this. This time it was not fear of the unknown, but fear of not knowing how to deal with it, not knowing how others would react to me with a handicapped child, of not knowing if I could handle taking care of a "special" child. I knew that it was not something contagious, or that it happened because of something that I had done, but what could I do about it?

How will my family react? These and other thoughts bombarded me as the doctor kept on explaining.

"Down's is a form of mental retardation that has various levels of learning impairments. It can range from severe retardation to living in society without the average person being aware that they have a learning disability. We won't know how severe the retardation is until she gets older."

I knew what the other symptoms were: a wrinkle line across the palm of the hand that extends from one side of the hand below the little finger to the other side of the hand; slanted eyes and extra epicanthal folds create a shape to their eyes that give them the appearance of the Mongolian race (hence the nick name); an extraordinary amount of space between the big toe and the second toe; and various commonalities in the genetic structure of the chromosomes, mainly on the twenty-first chromosome. One of the interesting characteristics of these people, which is rarely spoken of, is loving-kindness. My daughter is just such a person as this. She will come up to me in the grocery store, put her head on my shoulder, and say, "I love you, Mom. "

Some people react to these situations with fear, but others react with acceptance, rejection, or just indifference. My mother stood by me in the hardest of times. I was in the hospital when my sister came in to tell me that the rest of the family decided that it would be fine for me to let Sirena be adopted by someone else. Mother had already been admitted to the hospital to have a hemorrhoidectomy, so I called on the phone to her room. "How are you feeling, Mom?"

"The only time I feel good is when I've been sitting in the sitz bath."

"I know what you mean. Those little tubs sure make it easier to sit and make you feel better. Did Kathleen come in and see you?"

"Yes, she just left. She told me what they decided to tell you. How do you feel about it?"

"I don't want to rush her, but I can't seem to make them understand that. What are your thoughts on it?"

"As long as you want to keep her, then that's the thing to do. I'll stick by you and we'll make it work out somehow." For three days after, I had a hard time getting the rest of my family to realize that this was what I wanted to do, even if it wasn't what they wanted me to do.

Shortly after Sirena was first born, the doctor said she would probably not be able to walk until she was almost five years old. I can remember a question that kept running through my head, "Why me? Why right now?"

I now know the answer to that question. We have had to make quite a few changes in our lives to accommodate Sirena's handicap. There are many fringes where we have had to spend more on teaching, or on making arrangements for her future. Every learning experience, such as walking, tying a shoe, riding a bike, learning to read or do math, was the result of repeated efforts by many of our family, friends, and educators who had faith in her that she could achieve more than what we were prepared for, and she did.

She was walking and completely potty-trained by the time she was two and a half. But the impairments are still there. Learning is very difficult. It takes her patience to learn anything, and now we're seeing changes in the family that we had no idea would happen. One of my brothers, who I always thought was started coming over with little treats for her (usually candy); one of my nieces is a teacher for the handicapped, and another is taking courses for teaching them and has been working as an aide in a class for the

118

handicapped. All in the family will go out of their way to make sure Sirena is taken care of when she is around them. One of my nieces has made several outfits for Sirena, just because she wants to dye her things. The last outfit she made for her was a sweat suit adorned with hearts and bows, crafted from my father's handkerchiefs after he passed away, which were pasted onto the shirt and pants.

The reactions from my family have been very supportive since the decision was made to keep Sirena, but many times when people, who do not understand the syndrome, come upon Sirena, they poke at her or even are mean. At the age of twelve, she was already a very big girl because her favorite thing to do was eat, especially sweets. So, I would encourage her to be as active as possible, and one thing she used to enjoy doing was riding her adult-sized three-wheeled bicycle on the sidewalk up and down our road. After a few days, I noticed that she had not been taking her bike out on the sidewalk.

After coaxing her a little, I found out that one day, when she was riding her bike on the sidewalk, there was a loud crack like she heard at the fireworks, but it was under her bike and scared her. Someone had thrown a firecracker under her bike. This type of reaction by the general public is caused by a lack of understanding about the syndrome, which leads to difficulty in coping with the needs of the person and prompts them to keep their distance from individuals who have TMS retardation. If the person who threw that firecracker knew that she would never hurt them or their family, that what she had was not contagious, and that this was one of the few ways she enjoyed getting exercise, this adult would probably not have done this. However, there are others for whom I cannot find an excuse.

My neighbor called one day and asked, "Do you know what Sirena and Micah are doing?"

"I thought they were on the stone pile playing."

"I don't know what they are playing, but he is throwing stones at her."

That was the last friend Sirena had, a neighborhood friend to play with. Among all the neighborhood playmates Sirena had, we never found one who would play without hurting her, or who wouldn't break or steal her toys. One thing I find interesting is that rarely do I see these children telling their parents, "I love you." Is this something that is leaving our culture?

Even though there are many people in the world who react to mentally impaired people this way, there are many more who react differently. Our next-door neighbor, for example, when she sees Sirena sitting in the swing, playing her guitar, singing her favorite songs, and talking to her imaginary friends, will come over and bring any kind of treat for Sirena just to see her reaction and her smile. She doesn't even take the time to come in and talk to my mother or me, but she goes back home, and we will not know that she gave Sirena anything unless one of them tells us.

Often, I will know that Sirena has been given something because she will come into the house to throw the papers away and call out, "I love you, Mom." She knows she gets too many sweets, and she is encouraged to stay on a diet, but refusing them is hard for her to do, so she tries to hide the evidence.

Sirena has a charming smile that wins the affection of many acquaintances and changes the attitudes of many people. Even in church, when we first started attending, the members were very skeptical about us and would try to keep their children away from Sirena. I treat Sirena the same as I would a normal child. At that time, I made her attend Sunday school, and when she went to services, she had to behave and not run around. She participated in all the programs just like the other children, sang in the choir, ate at the social functions, and acted like the other children; therefore, it did not take long for the other members to learn that Sirena was not that much different from the other children in the Sunday school classes, and that she would not hurt their children.

Interestingly, the children never did notice a difference in her until they were much older, and she was always accepted by them. As a matter of fact, they remember her much better than they do me. One of the young members will see us in the store and come up to Sirena, talk to her, she will not recognize them if it has been over a couple of months since she has seen them, and then they will leave without saying anything to me, but Sirena will frequently come back to me and say "I love you, Mom." I sometimes wonder if this is because she is insecure, or because she does not understand why she does not know them.

Other people react with kindness. One such person is Marian at our local bakery shop. She loved to see Sirena come in there, because Sirena would patiently watch me as I would place an order for bread, never saying a word because she knew that if she begged to have me get something, she probably would not get it, but if she just stood patiently she would frequently get one of the many desserts there. Marian watched us come in there many times before she finally asked if it was okay for her to give Sirena her own bag of goodies—"just from Marian."

This went on for a while, and soon they were sending each other cards in the mail on special days. Last fall, Marian asked me what size shirt Sirena wore and said that she would like to dye her a special shirt. I had no idea what she intended, so when I saw the sweatshirt, I was really surprised.

She had counted-cross stitched Raggedy Ann and Andy on the front of it, and on the sleeve she wrote "Sirena" in stitching. This lady did not know us any differently than other customers, but she has become a very special person to Sirena.

There are many people in the world who will go out of their way to help those less fortunate than themselves, but there are still many who fear the unknown. We have come a long way in our society to help handicapped people by building schools for them, but we have not done very much to help others understand and overcome fears of handicappedness. In order to understand handicappedness better, we need to teach future generations to have more compassion, but more importantly, we need to teach them what it may be like to not be "normal." One way to address this issue would be to encourage more high school students to participate in foreign exchange programs, but this approach would be costly, and opportunities for such experiences are limited.

Another way to achieve a similar goal would be to have high school students visit and work on a weekly basis in nursing homes and foster homes. One concept is to give high school students a handicap, such as a blindfold or crutches, that they must wear for the day while they are in school. This exposes the student to the experience of these types of handicaps, but there is no way for them to experience mental retardation. There is no way for them to have this experience of true "handicappedness" unless they actually become handicapped.

I have never regretted keeping Sirena, and she has given all of us a new perspective on life that we never had before. We have learned to overcome our fears, to accept and enjoy what life has given us, and others have learned to overcome their fear and rejection of the handicapped. I would like to help others learn that there is nothing to fear from a handicapped person, and some of the ways for them to learn are very simple, but the handicapped people need many other people to support and initiate programs that help young people experience handicappedness.

There are many instances where a handicapped person is placed in what is called mainstreaming. When Sirena was placed in it, she was in the regular school system with normal children in the fourth, fifth, and sixth grades. The normal children would taunt the students from the class that was being mainstreamed. Other children repeatedly told Sirena to eat her lunch under the table, or when I monitored the lunchroom, I would find that the two paid monitors would stand off in the corners and not bother to watch the children in the cafeteria. They were too busy talking together in the corner of the room, while the students were throwing food across the room or tripping other students as they took their trays up to the conveyor. We need to initiate programs to encourage positive behaviors, not only for the employees but also for those supervising them, rather than pretending that problems do not exist.

# All Hallows Eve

I watch as she dons her costume with glee
Karate Kid with Roseann's roundedness.
"Trick n' treat" on her bag, Halloween spree
Candy on her mind, scaring folks with faces
"Aren't you a little big to be Trick or Treating?"

Next few years, costumes of ghosts, ghouls, and guns
Anxiously donned months before October
Viewed and praised only by near relatives
Special packages saved for someone dear
"Aren't you a little big to be trick or treating?"

"Remember, not all are as good and kind
As you would like. Don't fear the ghouls and ghosts,
Nor the witches and goblins, we do not mind,
Fear those who spike the candy and grab kids."
Sixteen going on seven, you don't understand.

"You must stay home and pass out the pencils."
"But I want to dress up in a costume!"
"You can if you stay at home tonight with us."
"Can't I go around Aunt Kathleen's home?"
Eighteen going on seven, you don't understand.

September: Karate Kid, November:

Still wearing Power Ranger's sword and hat.

Even in July, your costumes appear.

Anticipating Halloween evening.

Twenty going on seven, you will never understand why not.

The poems are mine

But the feelings and thoughts

Are universal to those who understand life

# Inner Journey

Words of sandy grit catch in my throat

Work has to be done!

I want to say NO!

There must be a

Time to go


A

Rose's

Enjoyment

Begins life again.

Clouds float in the sky.

Time now grows longer through the days.

# Jumping the Fence

Freedom! Jumping

on the brick fence

walking its length

you helping me

realize

I am

completely free. You

walking beside me,

laughing at my antics. I

can do what I want for

the first time. The gate

is open, taste the

world's air.

# Here's a Ticket

Our paths crossed for

a short time, but you

never realized I was

on the same road.


Your Defensive

Armor all but hid a

spark of a smile

within a heart.


My vulnerable coat,

Though new, it is weak;

a mere jacket a

sweater a toy


Our empowerment

like black and white

Shows you flying freely

But when I try

Here's a ticket!

# The Bench

Bitter

Pacing the pavement

No better than anybody else

Refusing to relinquish

Feelings

That broil


Benighted

Where to hide

Diesel stings my nose

Terminal looming ahead

Alone

No Shilo to help


Shyly

Pretending to belong

The bench soon becomes hard

Others lie

Soon I too

Lie

Dawn

Time to work

Nothing to change

Return in silence

Nothing worse done by me

Then what has been done to me


Glares "Where have you been?"

Silence

"You're right, I don't deserve an answer."

Strings unmendable

Dangling.

# Watermelon Belly

I pull myself up the bus steps in Los Angeles.

The driver looks down, "You're not delivering on my bus."
His frown spread like wild madness. Every driver glowered
their fear. Seeing the watermelon belly, their lips set.

Wanting separation. This butterball shape dumped. Then,
one did not see me get on. Three AM going toward Las
Vegas. Tired of sitting, I walk to the bus's front asking,
"Okay to stand here?" and we chat.

Talking to the mirror, "Where're ya goin'?"

"Saginaw, Michigan. " Dash lights glowing,

Reflecting on the window, "Where'd ya start?" 'Los
Angeles." Then he turns his head,

the watermelon belly obvious.

Whites of his eyes encircle huge dark disks. "No-No! Yer
Yer NOT!!!" His dark face glistens, reflecting headlights.
"What? Oh No! I'm fine! Don't worry." The bus tire slides
off onto gravel. "Please just watch your driving, I'm fine."

"The road is quiet..." I say anything, and return to my seat
to make him feel better. A few minutes later, he stops the
bus and says, "I need fresh air," then he runs into the
bushes! My face flushes.

# Nourishment Drained

A newspaper here

A bottle was left there

No one sees nor cares.

Minds as empty

As the last bottle.

Nourishment passed through

Our minds linked in distance

That should have been closed

When we went our ways.

But strings propped the door,

It remains open.

Nourishment drains

In fantasies no

Longer feasible.

# Survivor's World, 1993

I sit and watch with joy, this
creation of mine, as she sits
on the swing, holding the
world in her hands.

She comprehends the imaginary
friends storybook fantasies
and the joy of receiving gifts
and giving love.

How did I deserve this gift of
Love, more powerful than the
fear of dealing with one
exceptional human?

# My Special Child, 1974

Heaven sent me this special child.

Can I give all that I want to this special child?


Let me give her love, for love is a special child

Let me give it life, for you have not lived without a special child.


Teach me patience to be able to teach this special child.

Give me time to learn how to cope with this special child.


Help me, lord, with your little angel, my special child.

# Family Tree

Branches towering over

me, blue sky softening

harsh bark

Dog chasing

squirrel up the

tree.


I twist, swirl, furl

in upon myself,

falling within

remnants of last year's

foliage.


Scales balance heavy on

Pain, watching the process

withering and wrinkling

Aging generations

progress into

Antiquity, senility, finality.

Among ancient ancestors,

following a lonely

pilgrimage, through soft

Earth advancing vaults of

history, repeating patterns

of pain, joy of birth mixed

With death's pining.

# God's Mansion

# Pleasance

Holy Garden bridges life's span, she shouts silently amidst sounds: motors and Mankind.

Man's swollen heart rushes here, reluctant to go, leaving scars on Earth in refuge.

Lovers in search of solitude, mothers in search of solace, lonely ones reaching...

Dare I go on? As falling leaves float past the red wood railings, blocking the wet path.

Doors forever unlocked. Holy communion offered, tie and shoes not necessary.

Run up the embankment! Man's voice echoes wood planks rattling over murky water.

Reflections of naked branches mirror the soul against the soft, changing blue sky.

Mother provides, even when Man bleeds her, Father helps by preventing mankind's fall.

Splinters from the Table, reality painfully comes: musicians and jugglers.

Coats of vibrant colors, Nature's palette, Man's architectural creations. Live!

Evermore following paths, living lives in wonder, showing it is worthwhile for all.

Lovers in search of solitude, mothers in search of solace, lonely ones reaching...

Now green leaves speak, crisp fall air breathes in spite of trash cans, the soul swells and swells.

Silently, they sing, Untouchable Strings, an Orchestral performance of the World.

# Hesitancy

Bewildered, I stand here

Looking down off the hill.

Twenty years of

building.

Now, look around

Discover others,

Kings with power.

Keep building?

Like in the surrounding mountains?

But how?


That one over there

A tower on the side

Not the moat.

The power is exhilarating!


Intimidating.

The hill took time,

Hard work,

Tiring

More than I want to do

On a hill.

A hand holds out more clay.

It sparkles turquoise, emerald, ruby, and crystal

Pure and clean

My hill would shine,

Mix the colors,


Bend them into shapes. Add them

On the morning sun side, Grow!

# Steinbeck's Child

Velvet soft petals stretching up.

Perfect red buds from loving hands

Blooming from gentle, deep red hearts

Basking in glorious sun's rays


White, pure, sweet-smelling perfume

Lures nurturing lassitude till starvation

Vanity preserves rose's beauty with

gentle words and flattery


Finally hiding from the truth, acid

Rain falls on delicate skin

Blighting soft touches with holes

Petals fall, landing on callous

Hands


Steinbeck's Lenny pawing at frailty

shoving petals at a silent heart, horrified

as thin membranes melt underneath the

Hot Glue Gun's silent point

blood red rose fragments drip and

fall staining all things that it touches

leaving faded flat dead roses, who's

Sweet perfume is burnt plastic.

# Cocoon

Without ugliness, there can be no beauty.

Without hate, love is lessened, without clouds and rain,

the sun  stifles and suffocates,

Without tart lemons, there is no lemonade

The acrid healing drought kills


that empty void inside

Unable to be sated

With honey bread or sweet wine

Grows and engulfs the soul

Until it bursts like a water balloon


Nothing left inside

Nothing left to hide

Guts spilling out

From wounds no longer sewable

Remnants of junk food for carrion


Willfully withdrawing

Leaving pain to those who give

To those who do not care

Who or how they hurt

But victims shall remain


Wrapped within the gauze

Warmth and security lie

Blinded within the haze

Guarded from lies

Intended to hurt

Succeeds.

# Sparrow

Cold north wind ignores my feeble jacket

Tight back muscles begin painful spasms.

Twice a day, I walk through the long tunnel

That drains what little energy I have.

Concentrating and focusing on tasks becomes impossible
for my weak mind.


Genetics and disease shove me all ways

'Til in blind fury, my head breaks water.

White light radiantly flashes and blinds me,

Brilliant colored sparks drizzle through closed eyes,

Pristine beauty forever remembered:

Illumination of knowledge and understanding.


Fragmented pieces pulled from greater

Minds than mine, I combine in feeble

Disarray. Occasionally creative, I

build a small facsimile of art in poetry.

A shining gift radiating its cry

Drowning pain in soft, petaled roses and blue forget-me-
nots.

Like the fragile petals of baby blue

The muse's illumination withers.

In brown murky muddiness, my mind

swims without control, whipped around, and

around in the tunnel until stopped. My mind

lies

Like the sparrow that hits a window pane.

# Ages Pass

Winter nights now confine time in dank

walls, bitter nights feel longer within my

Mynde Wall's touch me

and leave me yearning for you. How close to force

Time and us are apart, Cloister me in loneliness

and oneness.


Ages pass and leave me out of life's time.

Change the wind as it moves, touching my

cheek would be easier to accomplish than to

right myself back into the right time. Now is not the age of
adventurers.


Pilgrims do not quest for Grails or passions,

Poets do not write in rhyme or meter,

Lovers do not remain in love; it dies.

Marriage is not an institution,

Families do not have moral values.


Out of synch in my time, I remain here

Within dank walls and tall stacks, my soul

turns, lacking resources to find love as it flies

to someone living time zone away.

I hide fearing painful memories.

# Sonnet

In empty rooms, some golden silence is seen;

But hearte, in loneliness a burden tende,

From paine eased, only Sirus who can mend,

With smiles and laughter, these are my wounds I see.

These wounds of time and loneliness are vilely

Opened by thee, who says is love and friend.

In times of need or hardship, lone intend to

Let thy sunne from thine eyes shine on me.


I forever give thee what here doth grow

Thou forever taking beyond my wan

Range, what oceans of delight in me doth

flow.

A handshake breaks the gap of land so

Strange, A kiss can heal a child's wee wounded

A hand, A hug, a smile, can stop the lonely stand.

## b

A day shall come when givers become haze

Whose hearte is empty, nothing left to feel;

From Virtue's patient silence left to deal,

Where my sad, lonely hearte is delayed daze

Of desire, for my heavenly love's gaze.

O Sirus! Musicke thy voice, my ears feel

Thy Eolian Harp strings, my heart doth reel.

Strange flames of Love in it our soules would raise,

Where breezes warble, changing mute still air

To words I know do well set forth my mynde.

But this does not ease my grievéd despair

Which never heeds the fruits of writer's kind.

A wounded heart still bleeds when pierced with darts

Of Cupid's bow, whose shaft did wound my hearte.

## c

With rage of Love, I called my love unkind

For in his hearte that ever there did raigne,

This sovereignty of my hearte he did

gaine;

I am resolv'd he hath no caring mynde.

I lodg'd thee in my hearte, and being blind

Did not see sweete regard for sharpest paine,

Then leaving me my error to maintaine.

For like a child that some faire book doth find,

The wit new got to play and falls to woes;

When I learned a lesson new have speld in deed;

To find in myself so foule, and stumbling so

That all my hurts in my hearte's wracke I reede,

Where Love's in want of joyless hopeless peace,

And I mad with fright, want wit to cease.

# Language, Life, and Learning

Deeper, further, behind I fall within
This whole world of language, life,
and learning. As the past abounds with modern
concepts, I see worlds that float in evolving
roles. Transitions of epochs spiraling deeper.

Arthur did not lose to Gawain in the war
Only to be born again in Spenser.
Later, I see myself falling again, needing
to be picked up, revived, in love.
Wanting, learning, thirsting for a pattern.

Rogers explains life as mankind changes
Everything is cut and dried in science.
Nothing left for imagination's art
Computers controlling and living
Lives for us as we are couch potatoes.

Revive! Alive in Love's discovery
Imagination lives in Canterbury!
A small footstep by a man is a giant leap.
man, in armor, brightening up the moon
As she goes on to the next eclipse.

# Prologue To The Canterbury Tales: A Tribute To Chaucer

There was an aged man with a young child

Whose hair was so thick, as if it were wild,

Hanging from his neck, tied and matted

down, as if no comb had touched his brown

crown.

The old man cared for him like a mother

The fact is, he was his great-grandfather.

The old man's beard was white as snow and long,

Nor was he such a one to give a song.

He never spoke a word more than was need,

As if weighing each word and paying

heed To never be disdainful, proud, or

Fine, as if in earlier life he lived on wine.

Never contemptuous of other men,

He was an honest worker, good without

sin, and steadily about his work he went,

And patient when difficulty was sent.

Hardy he was, handsome and bold of face,

As if age had given him special grace.

A great, wide fellow, big in brawn and bone

His head was like a block, his face brown toned.

His forehead was certainly fair in spread

Almost a span across the brows. With dread,

Almost hiding behind twinkling eyes, grief

Wrinkles around his mouth were strained as if

He cannot weep for all his inward smart,

For that which was most dear to his big heart.
Compassionate and kind he was, and would

For love hath no beginning nor end.

The child held in his lap like precious gems

Together they rode on a farmer's horse,

Reins held by the old man to keep in course.

Great-grandfather was old but steady of hand

To do their pilgrimage, render thanks, and

To pray for healing for the legs of the grandson,

Withered and shrunken beyond recognition.

# Chasing the Stream

Our paths crossed one day, doggedly

Footsteps following yours and the stream.

Confidently, you walk onward

While I run, catching

nightingale's.

Songs in clean air, then lured away

To visit Bandura or Aronson.

Steeped in riddles from Exeter,

I chase a rabbit down a hole.

While the stream flows, then branches,

You follow it to the right,

I cross through rapid water

Following it to the left.

We'll meet

again at the ocean.

# A Weg

I SAW a creature extending

As far as the eye could see, winding

It's many legs. Moving faster

In the daylight, but at night slows

And glows red and white, when the legs

Get tangled together, it can't move.

Appendages fall off and lie there, left behind

in a cloud of smoke.

It reproduces taking legs

From its side, going in circles,

Then leaves its parent, starting anew.

When it moves, it kills swiftly

Becoming fat and unmoving. If you

can saga hwæt hit is.

# Transcend

Climb,

Must, climb

Out of these

Deep Dead Letters.

No longer buried

Beneath piles of blinders

Look,

Look deep

With new sight

And perspectives

Forming, evolving

Growing, developing.

Shape,

Build forms

That scaffold

Worldly knowledge

That transcends in life

On a deep foundation

Fly,

Higher

With the wind

On shuttlecraft

Span the universe

See the Holy Garden!

# The Snipe Hunt

Such kind, gentle words

I believed them

Every one of them

"Wait for me," you said.


Loneliness settles

Nature and I hear

You are in the distance

"Will you keep your promise?"


The damp air settles.

With dew on my face

I stand alone here

My arms and the bag empty.

# Tiny Crying Baby

Do you hurt like I do?
Itchy bandages hold
Stopping any movement
Pulling every time eating
Or getting on bedpans.

Monsters in ash green suits
Walk in without faces.
Their needles and fingers
Probing, pulling burnt skin
Raw meat burns as air hits it.

Pain stops hours later.
Nights are long with noises
Your cry comes through the floorboards
Forcing the hurt deeper
Tiny crying baby.

Nurse's light probes the darkness
Startled by open eyes
"It's three a.m., you're awake?"
Why do they not hear you
Tiny crying baby?

# GRANDPA

When I was just very little, I remember sitting on your knee

And always there was your little smile, and the way you would tease me.

But then I grew too big, or your lap too small

You still always teased me, with that twinkle in your eye, and your face full of smiles.

You would put up your hands, as if you were going to fight with me.

It was our own way of greeting each other, you see

And to say, we are both in there fighting together

Now these precious memories will linger on forever

With a smile, a twinkle, and a tease.

# LIFE

The world is full of many things, but the most mysterious thing in this world is life.

Life! What is it? What does it consist of? Where does it come from?

From many men, we have many different answers.

Answers. Or are they answers? Each man in his own mind knows what is wrong and what is right.

Right for whom? For him! Only his answers are right for his problems.

Problems are a part of life, we learn to live with and to cope with them.

With each problem that comes up, we learn.

Learn how to walk, to run, to smile, to frown, to hate, to love.

Love, the greatest bond between men,

What has not been done for the sake of love?

Love is the never-ending light that guides our path through life.

Life is worth living when you can share it with someone.

Someone who can understand and be patient when we make mistakes, are angry, or we just don't know what to do.

Do you know that love is the greatest thing about life? I love you!

You make my life worthwhile. But because I love you, I never stand in your way for you to do as you wish.

Wish for happiness, and you won't get it unless you are doing what you wish for.

For I want you to be happy, so do as you wish, no matter what I say. Life is too precious to love without happiness.

Happiness, that is what I wish for you.

# GENE

You came into my life.

When despair was near at hand

Unknown to you, when you came to me for help.

You were helping me

As much as you say, I have helped you.

You have helped me more.

For living in this world without someone to love you

Is like living without a purpose.

My world is alive now,

My purpose is for you.

Let us not go astray from one another,

For this is where we belong,

Helping one another through

Life's misty dawn.

# Moon Beams

As the moon held me captive in the palms

of its beams,

I look down on the stars, whose eyes seem

to twinkle and gleam.

My mind seems to race with thoughts as I dream,

But I know that when the sun comes with its beams,

A new day will be dawning without my dreams.

Throughout the day, the sun holds me captive in the palms
of its beams.

Shining on the grass and the leaves on the trees, and the
water gleams.

But the nighttime comes again, and once again the moon
holds me captive in the palms of its beams.

# Time

Time: does it help?

They say it does

But how can it? Our feelings are still there.

Time: it only covers it up,

Covers it up so you can smile.

Smile for what?

Time. . . The need for love is always there.

When you love someone, you need their love.

Without it, life becomes unbearable again.

Time: It increases the need for you,

For without you,

Minutes feel like hours, and hours feel like days.

Time to think

To dream

To cry

Time: an endless entity

Empty and alone

By myself.

# HOME AGAIN

You are home again! But yet you're not?

Flying free like the wind through the trees

Like trying to catch the rays of the sun

As it slowly sets behind the trees.


You came quietly in the morning.

Your rays shine brightly on the dew on the grass

Creating smiles on everything you touch,

Giving it a beauty it's never shown before.


Then you go again, as your rays set with the sun

Giving everything big, dark shadows.

And soon, all too soon, there is no light here

Making the world as dark as it was before.


Then thoughts of you come back to me

Like the rays of the moon shining faintly through the trees,

Giving me memories of how beautiful yesterday was,

Praying that tomorrow will come quickly, and be more
beautiful than yesterday.

You must fly through my little bird,

And feel the beauty of your freedom,

For in the beauty of your freedom

Is the key to your success.

# Winged Birds of the Sea

Oh, how graceful they be

These winged birds of the sea!


Nothing can be more beautiful to see

Then their long necks and white ruffled feathers

against the deep blue sea.


None are better fishermen than they

Using their long necks to hunt for their prey,


And then as they fly away, their wings never sway,

These winged birds of the sea!

# LOVE

Love is like the shadows on the wall

Never real clear, and hiding little cracks


True love is without shadows.

All light shines so that repairs can be made on cracks.


But first, you must open your heart

To let your emotions be free to have true love.


Cracks can break a dam.

Think what they can do to a heart.


A heart that holds true love

Is very fragile.


If deep down in your heart

You don't really feel it.

It's not there

It is time to rebuild the dam.

Or else find another place to build

Where the foundation is firm.


Because without a firm foundation

That heart will break sooner or later.


Let it be never

For I truly love you!

# WHAT WILL HAPPEN NOW?

Time has changed us

Is it for the best?


Will we now find out

If we were meant to be?


You are not ready to be tied down

Am I?


I am afraid

Of losing you? Or of it not working out?


Time will tell us

What will happen now?

# The Great Majesty of our World

The great majesty of our world

never ceases to fascinate me.


The great trees reaching toward the

the sky is trying to catch the earliest rays

of the sun,


The birds are flying so gracefully as they

go about building and hunting.


All the animals scurrying about

making paths through the woods.


A world of majesty,

our world.

# HOW I FEEL FOR YOU

What can I say?

What can I do?

Except say I love you!


I know no other way

To let you know

To want you to know

How I feel for you.


There is no other way.

To explain what I do

Why do I cry for you?

For I love you.


What can I say?

What can I do?

Except say I love you!

# Music

Your beat has a way of lifting my spirits

It seems to ease its way into me

And change my whole feeling toward life.


When I'm down

You lift me up,

When I'm sad

You make me smile.


Music is the spirit of our hearts.

May it always be there to help those in need.

Let there always be music!

# IT IS TIME

It is time

The birds fly south

As they hurry about in their skelter.

Animals have gathered food and shelter

Preparing for these long and lonely nights.


It is time.

The leaves have been touched by Jack Frost

Providing a warm blanket for the animal shelter

Mother Nature has provided for her children during these
long and lonely nights.


It is time

For us now to prepare for winter's Frost

Closing our doors and windows to our shelter

And putting our hearts close together in our shelter

Loving on these long and lonely nights.


It is time

Winter is a time of closeness and friendship

A white blanket of shelter

And a stillness of shutters

A big, loving fire for these long and lonely nights

OH

TIME

WINTER

WHITE

WARMTH.

# Taiwanese Friends

As international peacekeepers,

your daughters expand cultural awareness to our

unworldly families in need of visions of other cultures.
Their acceptance of our traditions and customs,

foreign and inexplicable, amazes me.

Gentle and refined are these peacekeepers.


Tsaimeai's brave little heart accepted our culture

without reservation; even when we knew not what we

did offended without intending to. She smiles and

shares her culture, her insights, and her ideals.

A teacher, a friend, and a companion.


Jaimei's light shines in her musically creative

talents, with musical notes and gossamer wings

Creating a kaleidoscope of colors and emotions

floating in the air, swirling 'round

unknowingness and bonded tradition.


Eva, eldest, with her two children, bonds the families' and
worlds in sibling respectability and role modeling.

Leader of siblings, she inspires from a distance;

a glow of warmth transcending oceans.

Stand up proud, for these are your children. Through you as their role models, mentors, friends, and guides, they pass on your inspirational qualities, sharing their friendship and talents to worlds beyond yours.

# MY FRIEND

A friend is someone who is there when you need them

Someone who cares about you

And listens.

A friend is someone who can understand how you feel

Someone who knows you

And helps.

A friend is someone who helps you up when you are down

Someone who can make you smile

And cry.

A friend is someone whom you can share your thoughts with,

Someone who shares his thoughts with you

And thinks.

A friend is someone whom you can put all your trust into

Someone you can depend on

And rely.

A friend is someone who knows no mountain is too high

 No river is too deep.

Someone who will be there

And share.

A friend is someone who thinks of you before himself

Someone who gives without return

And forgives.

I am your friend.

Will you be mine?

# YOUR SECURITY BLANKET

You have been with me for a very long time
To know that you have been mine.


But now my little friend
With time and circumstances, we must bend.


You must put up your little security blanket
And take this time to forget.


That I ever existed
It is to be remembered.


In the sweet memories
Of the past and future moments.


To say it this way, I regret
For it is impossible for me to forget.


But I cannot live with the hurt
For in my heart
I know I will never be more
Than, just your security blanket.

# Turning Point

We all reach that long letter

That seems to stretch forever.


And we know that we would much rather

Go on the straight and easy road that leads ahead, but goes nowhere.


Some can run down that straight road

And fall into a gold mine and end up loaded.


Then some go that easy way and end up in the gutter,

Talking about the other.


Climbing that ladder appears so tall, and the fall...

And the rainbow ahead appears so beautiful…


But you can reach the end of the road and end up loaded.

The end of the latter is success, you know,


But it is not the gold that looks so new,

And security lies in the known,

But not in the golden.

# Growing Pains

The bird soared high in the sky.

My thoughts seemed to follow it and fly. Thinking of where
my life began to grow,

The seed that had inspired me so.


Like the flight of that bird

The growth of my life was hard;

An upward climb through winds and breezes

Encouraged by each ray of sun that frees us.


To guide us through each downpour, through each time we
feel poor.

To make us realize how rich we are

With all the smiles and how the sun's rays reach far.


And let us not forget that beautiful day

When we take time to pray

And thank God for what we have,

To give us courage to work through times both easy and
hard.

Inspire me, lord, to be like that bird,

to continue going until my voice is heard,

And I hear the angels in heaven singing.

Then I know I will have journeyed through this life willing.

# Love Is Worth It

We shared a love so tender.
That when it came time to part
I couldn't be put asunder.

Our love was made of tender
Feelings and emotions are all part
Of our minds that can't be put asunder

I shall always cherish those memories.
And the times that we had
As part of my life's diary.

You said that you were sorry.
To hurt the one you love
But remember, my darling.

In love, you cannot be sorry
For the beauty of love
Of our love, darling

Is something that was
worth every minute we
had together that we shared.

# SWEETHEART

On Valentine's Day, we think of the ones we love.
Sweetheart, I love you

It cannot be put down in words the reason why

Sweetheart, I love you

I cannot tell you often enough that

Sweetheart, I love you

So, on this Valentine's Day, I want you to know

Sweetheart, I love you

And 1 shall always be here when you need me because

Sweetheart, I love you

And as time goes on

So shall my love for you

www.ingramcontent.com/pod-product-compliance
Lightning Source LLC
Chambersburg PA
CBHW071330120626
46546CB00002B/502